Dixie

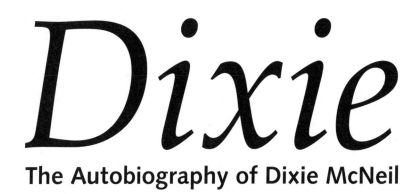

Dixie

The Autobiography of Dixie McNeil

Dixie McNeil
with Peter Read

This book is dedicated to my wife Dana,
sons Richard and Jamie, daughters-in-law Kerry and Teresa
and grandsons Jack and Morgan.

First impression: 2011

© Copyright Dixie McNeil and Y Lolfa Cyf., 2011

The publishers wish to acknowledge the support of
Cyngor Llyfrau Cymru

Cover design: Y Lolfa
Cover photograph: Rona Campbell
Wrexham football photographs courtesy of *Wrexham Leader*

Every attempt was made to ascertain and contact the source
of all the photographs in this book.

ISBN: 978 184771 365 0

Published and printed in Wales
on paper from well maintained forests
by Y Lolfa Cyf., Talybont, Ceredigion SY24 5HE
website www.ylolfa.com
e-mail ylolfa@ylolfa.com
tel 01970 832 304
fax 832 782

Contents

Foreword
by Graham Taylor

HAVING BOTH PLAYED with and then managed Dixie in the early 1970s at Lincoln City, I have fond memories of him as both a player and a man.

As a player his record is there for everyone to see: 239 goals in 522 appearances speaks for itself. Like all great goal scorers, he had no nerves when the ball came to him in the penalty box. He *wanted* to score, and if by any chance he didn't, it never affected his belief that he would score from the next opportunity – which he usually did.

Just as important was his attitude and approach in the dressing room. He was always one of the boys – a real team member. I have no recollection at all of Dixie acting in a manner where, because of his goal scoring abilities, he thought he should be treated in a special way. His feet were planted firmly on the ground.

I am sure that you will enjoy reading his story. I know that I will. Thanks for the memories Dixie!

Graham Taylor
former manager of the England Football Team

Foreword
by John Sillett

I CAME INTO Dixie's life through a meeting between Alan Dicks, Tony Collins and myself while at Bristol City Football Club. I needed to find a goal scorer, and Lincoln City FC had a player knocking goals in every week, so off I went to watch an evening midweek match at Leyton Orient. I reported back next day that I had found our man. Alan Dicks and Tony Collins watched him play two weeks later but, in their opinion, saw a different kind of performance. So, no deal! At the end of that season I left Bristol City and became manager of Hereford United FC. My first signing was Terry Paine. My next signing came about when the chairman Frank Miles and myself took off for Lincoln City and arranged to meet another young manager, Graham Taylor, who was in no way going to sell his star player. So Frank and I went to meet their chairman, and for £15,000 plus £5,000 if he scored 20 goals in his first season, we got our man.

Dixie was an honest and dedicated pro who trained very hard; he was quite stubborn with his beliefs, reminding me of someone I played with at Chelsea, Jimmy Greaves. I have no doubt that if he had had the chance to play in the First Division, he would have scored 25 to 30 goals a season with the right service. He had that great ability to score goals, but also good touch and vision and a wonderful understanding with Terry Paine, my player/coach, and with fellow striker Steve Davey.

Great players can be quite difficult to handle, but Dixie was without doubt a credit to his profession, a natural goal scorer who never panicked when in sight of the goal – his record speaks for itself. He was a class act, both on and off the field. If I had stayed at Hereford, he would have been the last player that I would have sold.

Dixie, my boy, you did me proud. It was a pleasure to work with you and you were one of the two best signings I ever made. Thanks for the many happy memories.

John Sillett
former manager of Hereford United FC
and Coventry City FC

Foreword
by Arfon Griffiths

WHEN I BECAME manager of Wrexham FC in 1977 we already had a good team but we needed a prolific goal scorer. The player we wanted was Dixie McNeil who, in my opinion, was the best goal scorer outside the then First Division. We paid £60,000 for him, which was a big fee for Wrexham. Dixie was worth every penny. We won the Third Division Championship and we also got to the quarter-finals of both League and FA Cup competitions. Dixie's goals were the reason for our success that season. Not only was he a very good player but a great character around the club.

He is a top man who, I am glad to say, is still a good friend to this day.

Arfon Griffiths
former manager of Wrexham FC

1

Beating a path to the Foxes

A POLISH DANCE in the village where my girlfriend Dana lived seemed like a good idea – a great way to spend a Friday night. Of course, things don't always work out in the best way and one problem was that I had an important football match the next day. Such worries seemed far away as one drink led to another. I probably had two or three pints and, anyway, the game was not until 3.00 p.m. the following day. It was at Edgerton Park in the centre of my home town, Melton Mowbray, where I would be playing for Leicestershire under-18s against Lincolnshire.

I guessed it would be a late night, so I left my mother a note telling her not to wake me until 12 noon. I explained I had a match in the afternoon and would want something light to eat, such as fish and chips. Polish dances are always lively affairs – they're not just a case of gentle jiggling around the dance floor. They involve polkas and all kinds of fast, complicated foot movements. The dance continued until 2.00 a.m. on the

Saturday morning, and I then had a two and a half mile walk home. My mother did exactly as I asked her, woke me at midday and then cooked me fish and chips.

I walked to the ground which was ten minutes from my house, arrived there at about half past one and prepared for the game. I was greeted by the other players in the team telling me that there was a rumour going around the ground that a Leicester City scout, plus other people from the club, were going to be present at the game. Such information went in through one ear and out through the other. The last thing I could imagine was that they were there to watch *me*. At that time I was playing regularly for the Holwell Works team in the Leicestershire Senior League. I played on the left wing and while I had bagged a few goals for the team, I had never given the idea of playing for a team from the top division of the English League a second thought. We played our match and won 5–4 in what, I suppose, you would call an open game of football. Playing as a youngster in a senior mens' team and not being particularly tall at the time, they had pushed me out onto the wing. Against Lincolnshire I ended up playing a deep midfield role. I managed to score one goal and on the Monday I received a message from the Holwell Works manager asking me to contact Matt Gillies, the Leicester City manager. He asked me whether I could play the following Saturday for their Reserves against Ipswich Town at Portman Road.

That Saturday, I arrived at Leicester station to travel with the team to Ipswich. I didn't know any of the team and I was quickly introduced to them before we boarded the train. I think we lost 0–1 on a pitch which was the most fabulous surface I'd ever played on. Even today, the

Portman Road pitch is one of the best in all the Football Leagues.

Without being outstanding, I felt I had played a decent a game against Ipswich Town. When I got back home there was another unexpected phone call telling me that Matt Gillies wanted to meet me. My Dad drove me across to Filbert Street on the Tuesday. As we chatted in the car, we assumed that he would say that he wanted me to play some more games for the Reserves. But, instead he gave us the incredible news that Leicester City wanted to offer me, seventeen-year-old Dixie McNeil, a two-year contract!

This was like a fairy tale. Since the age of twelve I had gone with my Dad to watch the Foxes. In the previous few seasons they had been one of the top teams in the First Division, which is now the Premiership. In 1961 and '63, they played in FA Cup finals against Tottenham Hotspur and Manchester United and the previous season they'd finished fourth. I had seen them play top European teams such as Atletico Madrid in the Fairs Cup, and I had also seen the Blackpool team with the legendary Stanley Matthews, who was still playing in his fifties. I couldn't believe that I was going to be a professional footballer for a team full of my heroes, who I'd followed for the past five years. I would be at the same club as Gordon Banks, arguably the best goalkeeper in the world, Derek Dougan and Graham Cross, who also played professional cricket for Leicestershire, and Jack Rowley a Leicester legend who just kept scoring goals year after year.

Whilst I was in my fairy tale world, Dad brought us all back down to earth. Matt Gillies was offering me

£20 a week, but Dad refused the offer. As an apprentice electrical engineer, earning £2.7s.6d. a week, £20 sounded like a fortune to me, but Dad insisted on £25, claiming that the extra £5 a week would go towards the cost of catching the train from Melton Mowbray every day. I discovered later that Dad's negotiating skills meant that I was earning £5 a week more than Peter Shilton, the future England goalkeeper who, at that time, was understudy to Gordon Banks.

My career with Leicester City didn't get off to the best of starts. In a training session, I sprained my ankle after a follow-through tackle from Len Chalmers, the first team's right back. Len was a no-nonsense defender, who broke a leg in the FA Cup final defeat to Spurs in 1961. He bore the distinction of being the last player to be carried off in a final, before the introduction of substitutes. Down to ten men for a long period of the game, Leicester had lost the match 0–2.

When I hobbled into the treatment room the physiotherapist asked, "How did you do that?"

"Lenny Chalmers," I replied.

The physio shook his head knowingly. "That's normal," he said.

Lenny obviously felt he owed it to aspiring footballers to teach them the rough side of the game and toughen them up.

Of course, there were glamour moments being on the books of such a top side. Every Friday, Gordon Banks who for some reason was nicknamed Sugar, would ask for two or three of the Reserves to go onto the pitch with him. The idea was that we were to take shots from the edge of the box. In reality, I suppose we weren't expected to hit the ball as hard as possible but, being confronted by the best goalie in the world, meant that I would always hit it as hard as possible, so that I could score past this amazing shot-stopper. Needless to say, he was so good, we hardly ever got past him.

The glamour continued as I travelled away with the Reserves. On the train our food was served silver service. This was a new experience for me, a boy brought up in a rented terraced house. It was also incredible to be served chicken frequently. For me, chicken was only ever eaten at special times of the year, such as weddings or Christmas celebrations. Feeling slightly out of place I tried to eat in a prim and proper way, taking the meat off the bone with my knife and fork. It wasn't easy and, towards the end of the season, I was relieved to see that all of us were using our fingers.

The most tense day of the week was always a Friday. We would wait for an hour or sometimes longer for the team sheets to go up. First teamers and Reserves would all anxiously gather around to see if they were playing the next day. One day, one of the players, Clive Walker, looked at the team to play Spurs Reserves at White Hart Lane.

He turned to me and said, "Do you realise they've got eleven internationals in their Reserve side?" Next day we played against a team of household names including Will Brown, the goalkeeper, Cliff Jones, the Welsh international winger and Bobby Smith the centre forward. These were all players who had starred in the great double winning side of 1960–1 season. At half-time we were holding this great team 0–0, but forty-five minutes later we had lost 0–6.

My time in the Reserves was a fantastic experience playing against amazing players such as the Allchurch brothers, Len and Ivor, of Swansea. But, I found it impossible to break into the first team. My position was taken by Mike Stringfellow. He was a giant of a man, all six foot two inches of him, who never got injured and had far more pace than me.

Although stuck in the Reserves, I never slipped into the A or B team. That was something to be proud of, and I was thrilled to be involved in such a professional set-up. The contrast in life, before signing and now, was unbelievable. The previous year I would be up at 6 a.m. in the morning to catch the bus for work, which started at 7.30. Then, after a hard day's slog at the factory, I'd catch the 5 p.m. bus and wouldn't arrive home for another hour. After gobbling down some food I would get to Holwell for training from 7 p.m. to 9 p.m. Two nights a week I would go straight from work to the local college, because I was an apprentice and had to study for exams. On those evenings, I wouldn't get home until well past 11 p.m.

So, the life of the professional footballer suited me fine. Which is why, when I was told at the end of my second season that Leicester City no longer wanted me, the news came as a terrible shock. I was devastated. Looking back I wonder if I was too young, too naive to read the signs. Perhaps I was too taken up with the fairy tale lifestyle to realise that during my time at Filbert Street, I probably struck the management as a 'Steady Eddy' player rather than as a footballer who was going to set the top division on fire.

As the news sank in, I began to wonder if I had

made the right decision. At the age of seventeen I had abandoned the possibility of an apprenticeship and education and chosen football. Perhaps I had made that decision even earlier in my life. At the age of eleven I had sat the 11+ exam and, as a border-liner, I was sent to Melton Mowbray Grammar School for an interview. To this day, I still wonder whether the fact that I ended up in the secondary modern school had more to do with one answer I gave at interview, than with my academic abilities. Looking at me, the Headmaster asked what I wanted to do with my life. I answered him immediately, "a professional footballer". Walking out of the gates of Filbert Street for the last time, I was left to wonder whether that was such a clever answer. The omens were certainly not good. Lots of careers finished at twenty-eight and many stars ended up running pubs.

I was now out of work. It was the mid 1960s and in those days footballers didn't have agents. I was very definitely on my own and wondered whether I could face the rest of my life with this kind of uncertainty. Not only were there no agents but there were no mobile phones either. And in my case, there was no landline at my parents' house, so I had to make enquiries about my future from public call boxes.

Eventually Exeter City of the Fourth Division contacted me. Their manager, Jock Basford, called me for a week's trial. Despite all the self-doubt and questioning since my Leicester exit, I packed my boots and headed for Exeter. I still had belief in myself.

2

A millionarie in Exeter and danger in Corby

JOCK BASFORD HAD decided that the only way to get out of the Fourth Division was to sign players from First Division clubs. Most of them had been released without making the grade as an established first team player. In addition to looking to Leicester for my services, Basford also got players from clubs such as Charlton Athletic and Arsenal. It meant that the Grecians had one of the youngest teams in the division, with an average age of twenty-one. Possibly one of his most famous captures was that of Ray Harford, who later was to become a well-known and respected coach at the highest level.

At the end of my week's trial I was signed by Exeter. They wanted me to play as an out-and-out striker, unlike my wider role at Leicester. I moved down from Melton Mowbray. It felt like a million miles away from home, although I was made to feel extremely welcome by my hosts, who were a fairly elderly couple and, at times, it felt like living with grandparents. I've no idea what they made of Ernie, my roommate, and his choice of music.

Ernie was also on Exeter's books, and shared the digs with me. When we returned to the house after training, he would play the same music every afternoon. He was seriously into heavy American rock, which would make the house shake every time I tried to relax. I just hope that the couple were hard of hearing.

The house was near the river Exe and, with its cathedral, parks and friendly people, I came to like Exeter very much. St James' Park attracted crowds of around 5,000 for most games, and the ground is one of those places that every time I return, I feel it will never change. With all the trees surrounding one side of the ground, it feels quaint and friendly.

I made my first appearance as a professional footballer on the opening day of the 1966–7 season. At the time I did not realise the irony that my first game was against Wrexham at the Racecourse ground. Later in my career, I would be involved in the Welsh club's greatest season, and was to grow close to the fans and settle in the town. The game ended in a 0–0 draw. With a few minutes left, I was put through on goal, but hit the post at the Mold Road end of the ground. I now look back on that miss and give a huge sigh of relief that I didn't score.

One of the biggest problems playing for Exeter was that, apart from Torquay United, there was no such thing as a local derby. For almost all of our away games, we had to leave on a Friday morning and stay overnight. There were several eight-hour journeys to places such as Carlisle or Workington. I can still feel the dread of the bus hitting the outskirts of Bristol at midnight on a winter's evening, realising that there were still two more hours to go before arriving home.

Those buses were alright, but they were hardly luxury coaches. There were no televisions and no music. For lots of the players, the only way to relieve the boredom was to play cards on the journey to and from the match. What they lost heading north, they would try to win back, heading south. At the heart of the betting syndicates was a very talented left back called George Ley. In the close season, England had hosted the World Cup, which of course they went on to win. George had used his gambling knowledge to great effect and scooped massive winnings. It was little wonder that he was keen to play on every trip. For a young boy from Melton Mowbray, the whole culture of a professional football club was a huge eye-opener.

As well as growing used to long journeys, I had to make a major decision with Dana. Before I had moved to Exeter we'd become engaged. With my constant travelling and commitments to the club, it became increasingly difficult to see Dana in Melton Mowbray and, because of the huge distance involved, it was difficult for her to get down to Exeter to see me. We were both aware of the hardship of long distance love and, from our knowledge of other people's lives, it never seemed to work. In view of this, we decided we would marry and that Dana would join me in Exeter.

I discussed the situation with the club and we fixed 2 January 1967 as the date for the wedding, which was a Monday. I was left in absolutely no doubt that I had to be back in training first thing Wednesday morning. It was all a far cry from today's Premiership players – many of whom are given a fortnight off to solve a domestic. So, after a one-night honeymoon in London, Dana and I returned to Devon where we moved into a one bedroom bedsit for £5 a week.

Like many people at that time, we would try our luck on the Littlewood's Pools every weekend. One Saturday, Dana was checking the scores as they came up on the TV screen. We already had five draws selected and to be a millionaire you needed eight. We had chosen three more, all of them in the Scottish League. The first one came up as a draw, and so did the second. We were on the brink of flash cars and luxury homes! One more result to come. Up it came. It was a draw. When I returned home from playing football, Dana showed me the results and I realised we were in the money.

When we came to collect our winnings we realised that our dreams of millions had been slightly misplaced. We had won the princely sum of £60, which was just three times what I earned each week. It was a nice bonus, but I knew I wouldn't be getting my saloon car.

At the end of the season I was fairly pleased with my first stint as a professional footballer at Exeter. The team, which was very young and inexperienced, finished fourteenth and I'd bagged eleven goals in thirty-one appearances. With six games to go, manager Jock Basford was dismissed and replaced by Frank Broome. At the end of the season Broome shook my hand and said, "See you next season."

During that first season in the Football League I sustained my first serious injury. In one of the games a stone flew up and gashed my knee, and I needed six stitches. Nowadays, players are rested, but in the 1960s you were rushed back into action. Besides, players were desperate not to lose their £5 a week appearance money.

If I am invited to give an after dinner speech, I often begin by saying:

> After eighteen years as a professional footballer, my career has been relatively injury free! However, I have torn my left calf muscle and right thigh muscle, broken a finger, my cheekbone, collarbone and broken my nose three times. I have fractured my skull and my ankle bone. In a FA Cup match against Blyth Spartans, I tore the tendon in my foot and had five cortosone injections in a few days. Other than that, I have come out of professional football relatively unscathed!

At Exeter there was now the summer to recover and come back refreshed for the new season. Or so I thought. Then, the bombshell dropped through the letter box. Frank Broome – who had shaken my hand, smiled and told me he would see me next season – was now writing to say that my services were no longer required.

I was absolutely devastated. I couldn't understand why, after a return of one goal in every three games, the club was getting rid of me. All the old doubts which had lingered in my mind when I left Leicester City, came back to haunt me. Was I good enough? After all, here I was twice in one year being placed on a free transfer. Dana and I went back to stay with my parents in Melton Mowbray. Twelve months on I was faced with the same difficulties as when I had left Leicester. It was a long trek to the phone box to chase a club. I had letters of interest from a few teams and Chesterfield definitely wanted to sign me.

It was time for another long hard think. The more Dana and I discussed the situation, the more obvious it became that the only solution was to combine a full-time job with a semi-professional club. And that is why I went for the option of Corby Town, the Southern League club. Their manager was Tommy Haddon, and he offered me £10 a week for the football, with £4 a week for the summer, plus a job in the steelworks as a painter. As Corby was only an hour's drive away from Melton Mowbray, and Chesterfield was much further away, the decision struck me as a 'no brainer'.

So, one Monday morning, I went to the steelworks in Corby with fellow player Mick Addy from Leeds. The club had done a similar deal with him. Mick was a great midfield player and really should have been playing in the Football League. Playing football matches he was very comfortable on the ball, but I'm sure that as we walked into that building, like me, he felt anything but comfortable. We were told to go to the far end of the building and ask for the foreman of the furnaces. When I saw where we would be working, I couldn't believe it. Surely this was some kind of joke?

Suspended two hundred feet in the air was a wooden structure which would lead us to twelve-inch-wide girders. The plan was that we would lie on these and paint the ceiling. There were no safety ropes and nothing to catch us if we fell. Our job also entailed painting the pipes that went into the furnaces and the chimneys. Also, we had to operate jack hammers inside the pipes, so that the vibrations would dislocate the bricks. Sometimes people look at me, smile, and then say, "You are so lucky, you've had it so easy." When they say that, I just stare back and say, "No I bloody well haven't."

Three days into our new job, Mick and I came down off the girders for our lunch. We wondered where all the other painters were and, on asking, received an amazing answer. They had been told that they could knock-off early. They had been painting, and were found at the bottom of the chimney, gassed by the fumes from the furnaces. They were all asleep and so the management had woken them, given them a cup of tea and sent them home.

It left me wondering what had I done. The last couple of years had not been filled with the best decision making. After eight weeks I was moved into the offices and never saw a paint brush again.

On the football field things didn't go too well and Corby Town were relegated. In my second season at the club I was moved from midfield and asked to play as an out-and-out striker. The switch worked and I finished as top scorer with over forty goals. Nearby Northampton Town had obviously kept tabs on my progress throughout the season, and they bid £5,000 for me, which the non-league club accepted. I was on my way back into the Football League.

3

Mixing with the great – George Best and Graham Taylor

When I joined the Cobblers, they were in something of a state. It was 1969 and they were languishing in the Fourth Division. In the previous season they had scored less than forty goals and were obviously desperately in need of a striker. As I prepared for a new term with them, it was difficult to believe that just four years earlier they had been anticipating their first game as a First Division club, away to Everton. Prior to that game, they had raced through the divisions and risen from the fourth to the top flight in four seasons. Sadly, when I signed for them, they had made the return journey from First Divison to Fourth Division almost as quickly.

The manager was the Welshman Dave Bowen, who had taken the club up and down on their magical journey. He was also the manager of the Welsh national side. I found it difficult to take to him, and felt he wouldn't give me a chance in the first team. I moaned and groaned at Dave and begged him to choose me instead of his preferred striker, John Fairbrother. On one occasion I told the manager that I couldn't understand why he was selecting him ahead of me, because Fairbrother had hit the post seven times in his last nine outings. Dave Bowen interpreted that statistic as suggesting that any minute Fairbrother was going to hit the back of the net, and his goals tally would start shooting up. *I* interpreted it as proof that Fairbrother was not a better striker than me and Dave should send me on.

I also have to admit that his coaching left rather a lot to be desired. He told me, "All you have to do is put yourself in the right place and you'll score goals." Just as his coaching can be questioned, so too could his care of injured players. In 1971, in a pre-season friendly against the German team Hanover 96, the German keeper was anything but friendly, and kicked me in the head. When I came off at the end of the game, I realised that I could only move my mouth up and down. It was impossible to move it from right to left. When I shared this problem with Dave Bowen, he told me to return to the ground in the morning and report to the club physiotherapist. As well as the problem with my mouth, it soon became obvious to the physio that there was a large dint in my head where the goalie had kicked me. The next day, Thursday, I was sent to the hospital and was told to return the following day, when they inserted a large blade through my gum, to adjust the skull which was severely decompressed. I had to report back for training the following Monday. The next day Dave Bowen decided that I should do some gentle jogging. This continued for the rest of the week and then he told me on the Friday that he wanted me to play against Cambridge the following day. I explained that I had just had a fairly serious injury and operation and felt I should not play. His reply amazed me. "Don't worry, the problem is on the right hand side of your head. Just make sure you head the ball on the opposite side."

During my first season at Northampton I struggled to get into the team but did have the satisfaction of scoring the winning goal against Exeter City in a Cup replay. It is strange how footballers always get fired up in games against their old clubs. It is as if we have a point to prove. After Leicester got rid of me, I always wanted to go back there and play well to prove them wrong. I obviously wanted to make a point to the Devon club and years later, when I played at St James' Park for Wrexham, I scored the only goal in a game which the *Wrexham Evening Leader* reporter, David Lovett, described as 'Day Light Robbery'.

For me, the highlight of my first season at the County Ground has to be the club's run in the FA Cup. Our 2–1 victory over Exeter in the second round, came at Swindon's County Ground in what was the second replay after a 1–1 draw at home and a goalless draw at St James' Park. The earlier round saw us beat Weymouth 3–1 away. After a 1–0 away victory over Brentwood Town, we travelled to Prenton Park in the fourth round to take on Tranmere Rovers. We managed a draw, which meant that at lunchtime on Monday, we all huddled around the radio to see who we would play if we could beat the Wirral outfit. We couldn't believe our luck when it was announced that in the fifth round we would play Manchester United. This was the Manchester United of George Best and Bobby Charlton, the Manchester

United who, a few years earlier, had destroyed Benfica in the European Cup final.

The County Ground was packed to the rafters for our replay, which we won 2–1. Needless to say, for all the games leading up to the Cup tie we played in front of packed grounds, as the club introduced a voucher system for tickets to see the clash with Manchester United. When I think of the vast sums of money offered to today's footballers for big matches, it is incredible that, despite all the media attention both before and for the big match, none of our players were offered TV appearance money. We were told that if we beat them, we would be given bonuses of £20 each, or £10 for a draw. Otherwise, we would just be drawing our usual wages. In the event, we managed to negotiate with the club that we would get the programme money.

The match, which was played in early February, was a total sell-out and, at the gates, the club took record receipts. There were high points and low points during the game. The high spot was that I scored against one of the greatest teams in Europe. Another was that I played on the same pitch as Bobby Charlton and George Best. I suppose the low spot was that George scored six times and with two other goals from Bryan Kidd – the 2–8 result made unhappy reading.

After the match the chairman stormed into the changing rooms. Red with anger he told us that we were a total disgrace and the worst team that had ever played for Northampton. Once he had left, a mini rebellion broke out. We had tried our hardest against a great team and managed to score two goals. The players decided they were not going to accept such an outburst.

A few of them even talked about leaving. Two of the more senior players, Frank Large, and club captain, Frank Rankmore, decided that they would challenge the chairman. He apologised on the Monday, and a sort of calm was restored.

I battled on for a couple more seasons at Northampton. When we played Manchester United we were fourth in the league, but after that Cup thrashing we slipped down the table. In the first half of the 1971–2 season, although the team struggled, I managed to score fourteen goals. In January, I moved to a club nearer to the top of the table, when Lincoln City signed me, and in the second half of the season I found the net another thirteen times, so that I finished with twenty-seven goals.

The manager at Lincoln City was David Herd who, of course, made his name as a Manchester United forward. Sincil Bank was his first managerial post. I found him extremely helpful and supportive of my style of play, but I couldn't help feel that he missed being a top player himself. Every morning, when the rest of the team and I arrived at the training ground, we would see the familiar sight of David Herd, or Hurdy-Gurdy as he was affectionately known, smashing footballs into the back of the unguarded net.

In addition to the manager there was one other Red Imp player who became famous. A certain Graham Taylor, who was to go on and manage the England team. In a match at Northampton, Graham kicked the ground instead of the ball and seriously injured his hip. In a strange way, I believe that that injury led to the demise of David Herd and shortly afterwards Graham was appointed as manager.

After a match against Colchester, in which we played badly, Graham showed the tenacity that would make him a top manager. He kept us in the changing rooms for an hour and a half and read us the riot act. I knew then that he would make it big as a manager.

In the two full seasons I played for the Red Imps, 1972-3 and 1973-4, I finished as the club's top scorer, scoring twenty-one and nineteen goals respectively. At the end of the second season, we discovered that Dana was pregnant with our first son, Richard. Everything suggested it was appropriate to go and ask the manager for a pay rise of £5 a week. I had been the top scorer for the club for two seasons and Dana and I were expecting an addition. Besides, I couldn't think of a nicer person to approach for a rise, as we both considered Graham a very close friend. He told me that he would put my request to the Board of the club. It wasn't very long before he came back to me and said, "Sorry, as a club we're skint" and placed me on the transfer list.

During pre-season training for the 1974-5 season I, along with all the other players was distracted by the appearance of two large gentlemen, dressed in dark suits and wearing shades watching us. Despite all the guesses flying around at the training ground, it turned out to be John Sillett, the manager of Hereford United and his chairman Frank Miles.

The next day Graham called me into his office and explained that Hereford were offering £15,000 for my signature, plus another £5,000 if I scored twenty goals. Bowcock, the chairman of Lincoln City was resigning and the club owed him £20,000. I was obviously the cash cow.

John Sillett was offering me 50 per cent more wages than Lincoln, and so I think he was slightly surprised that I asked for forty-eight hours to consider his offer. Richard was still a baby, and it meant that this new approach from another club could cause tremendous upheaval for us and it would also mean hunting for a new house. But, after a lot of discussion, Dana and I decided to move to Hereford.

4

A lot of Bulls and George Best again

I JOINED HEREFORD United, the Bulls, at the beginning of the 1974–5 season. They were a new team to the Football League and, despite the fact they had only just escaped relegation to the Fourth Division, optimism around the ground and the town was high. Two years before I joined them, they had been a Southern League club who had provided the shock of the FA Cup with a 2–1 home victory over First Division Newcastle United. At the end of that season, despite finishing second behind Chelmsford, they were elected to the Football League to replace Barrow. In that first season, they finished second and were promoted to the Third Division. Colin Addison, who had guided them to these heady heights, was sacked at the end of the 1973–4 season. John Sillett, who had been coach at First Division Bristol City, replaced him.

The fans and most of the staff were still in dream land. It was difficult to believe that they had finished their second season as a Football League club with gates averaging around 9,000 fans per game.

My first senior football club, Howell Works FC in the 1963 Leicestershire Senior League Division 1. I'm in the front row, second from left

Leicester City youth team in Amsterdam in 1964 for a youth tournament. I was voted player of the tournament. Peter Shilton is in the centre, one row back

Northampton Town FC 1967. I'm standing in the back row, third from left next to a young Phil Neal who later played for Liverpool

Lincoln Imps: Ian Branfoot, Denis Leigh, John Ward, John Worsdale and me

Hereford United FC 1975–6

Playing cards on the Hereford United bus: Colin Lee, me, John Sillett and Dudley Tiler

Newspaper cutting from the *Wrexham Evening Leader* in 1977 just after I signed for Wrexham for £60,000

Wrexham Town FC 1977–8
Back Row L–R: Terry Bates, me, Bobby Shinton, Alan Hill, Dai Davies, Eddie Niedzwiecki, Wayne Cegielski, John Roberts, Les Cartwright, Norman Wilson (secretary)
Front Row: George Showell (physio), Alan Dwyer, John Lyons, Mickey Thomas, Arfon Griffiths (manager), Gareth Davies, Graham Whittle, Mickey Evans, Mel Sutton

And we dress up nicely too!

With Arfon Griffiths after winning the *London Evening Standard* Player of the Month

Wrexham FC First Team and Directors 1981–2

Under Mel Sutton and Mickey Evans, Wrexham FC after Arfon Griffiths

Wrexham winning the Welsh Cup against Kidderminster in 1986
Back row L–R: Luke Chadwick, John Gregory, George Showell, Frankie Jones, Jim Steel,
Ted Edwards, Dai Davies, Mike Williams, Neil Salathial, me
Front row: Paul Comstive, Steve Charles, Shaun Cummington, Barry Horne, Steve Buxton

A Dixie header at the Racecourse

At full stretch

Great left footer for a goal against Charlton

Taking a penalty at the Racecourse

Scoring a goal for Hereford United at Edgar Street against Grimsby Town

Scoring against Newcastle United in an FA Cup replay

Be brave – put your head where boots fly

Three Leyton Orient
players stand and
watch!

Les Cartwright,
Micky Vinter and me
celebrate a goal

Close marking to win the ball

Scoring a first-minute goal at home to East German side Magdeburg in the Cup Winners' Cup

That sweet feeling after scoring a goal

Heading the ball back the way it came!

The FA Cup against Bristol City. It ended 4–4 and I scored my best goal ever with my head

Right foot! Who can't kick with it! Playing in a match againt Barnsley

Newcastle United's Steve Carney pointing the finger for some reason!

Referee David Scott and me seeing things differently on a foggy day

"Don't agree
with that
one, ref!"

Best gunslinger in town! Walsall's Alan Buckley and me shoot it out to be the Football League's top goalscorer. Sorry Al, I won

The downside of professional sport. Crocked at the end of the season at the mayor's reception to celebrate that Wrexham are Champions of the League in 1978–9

The atmosphere of sheer excitement and self-belief around Edgar Street was one of the reasons I was keen to join the club. But the two most important factors were John Sillett and Terry Paine. Sillett obviously had great belief in my ability and I discovered that, whilst at Ashton Gate, he had wanted to sign me for First Division Bristol City, but manager Alan Dicks had been opposed to the move. John had watched me play for Northampton, returned to Bristol and had told Dicks, "I've found the one." Their disagreement over signing me was a major factor why John left Ashton Gate, and once he got to Edgar Street he was determined to have me on the books.

John was a larger than life character who, in the late 1980s, was to be remembered forever for his jig on the Wembley turf after Coventry City defeated Spurs in the FA Cup final. He ruled the team and the club with a rod of iron. If you stepped out of line you would be in big trouble. He was never afraid of humiliating you in front of the rest of the team, and yet, at the same time, he was a tremendous support and friend and would often take you out for a meal after he had read you the riot act. He was very much a man's manager and got the best out of his players. Most of the players were scared of him *and* loved him at the same time.

When we spoke, prior to me leaving Lincoln City, John certainly sold me the idea of joining the Bulls. In addition, there was also the prospect of playing with Terry Paine. Terry had played in the top flight at Southampton, making over 700 appearances for them, which was a club record. He had also been in England's World Cup winning squad of 1966, playing in the first game against Mexico. Although fairly small, weighing in at just nine and a half stone and five foot eight inches tall, he was incredibly tough and difficult to knock off the ball. He was also a great playmaker, and it was good to play in the same team as such a fantastic professional. On the wing, Hereford had Welsh international Bryan Evans and, with a mix of players who had come up with the club from the Southern League, plus players John Sillett signed, such as Irish international Terry Byrne and Peter Morgan, the Bulls had the makings of a strong Third Division outfit. After the problems I'd encountered at Lincoln after asking for £5 a week more, I was amazed and delighted to discover that I was on the same wage as Terry Paine, which made us the highest paid footballers at the club.

I was pleased to get on the scoresheet in my first game for my new club. Playing at home, we beat Aldershot 2–0 and I got the first goal just before half-time, with Kemp scoring the other. It turned out to be a fairly strange season with the club finishing twelfth. Our away form definitely cost us, as we won only twice, at Colchester United and Gillingham. Our home form, on the other hand, was superb. We won fourteen games, drew six and lost only three games. On 18 September 1974 we beat a Crystal Palace side which included Terry Venables in their line-up. This started an impressive run of form as we went undefeated at home in the league for fourteen games, nine of which were won.

Four days before Christmas, Blackburn Rovers, who were to be promoted as champions, came to Edgar Street. They boasted one of the best defences in the league and had never conceded more than two goals in a game. The boss didn't always give a lengthy pre-match talk, but on this occasion we were all getting worried as he sat us all down and talked to us for ages. He filled us with fear as he went through each of their players one by one, and more or less told us that they were the best in that position in the league. According to John, they had the best midfielders, the best goalie, the best strikers and so on. That day we played out of our skins and, with ten minutes to go, we were 6–1 up, but Rovers pulled two back to lose 3–6.

When I signed for the Bulls, they paid Lincoln £15,000 with a promise of another £5,000 if I scored twenty goals in a season. In this game I had already scored twice from the penalty spot and once in open play to get my hat-trick. This meant that in just four months at the club I had already scored eighteen goals. When we were given another penalty later on in the game, Frank Miles, the chairman, ran to the touchline and shouted, "Don't let him take the penalty. If he scores, it'll cost us seven hundred and fifty quid."

In March, after an away defeat at Bury, a 3–0 drubbing, John Sillett was furious. He stormed into the dressing room and said he wanted us all on the bus by 5 p.m. Like dutiful and naughty school children, we filed onto the coach and waited. And waited. And waited. He eventually got on at 6 p.m., having made his point. As we drove through one of the towns on our homeward journey, John decided that we should stop at a pub. Once we were all inside, he held court at the bar and pulled out his wallet. "I'm only buying for those who deserve a drink."

He looked around his team. "You can have one and you, and you and you", he said nodding at Steve Emery, John Leighton, Terry Paine and Dudley Tyler. Then he caught my eye. "Don't think you're getting one", he said. He gave the same treatment and message to goalkeeper Tommy Hughes, who had conceded three goals and to left back Tony Byrne. We were the only three singled out for criticism. "You are the elder statesman of this team", he said to me, "and so you should be setting an example on the field all the time."

Despite the fact that we were all scared of him, deep-down we all loved him. In spite of all the bollockings we received sometime in our careers, we knew that when he walked into the dressing room he would support us.

Very often when we were doing long-distance running around the pitch at Edgar Street, the window of his office at the side of the pitch would open and we would hear his booming voice echo around the ground, shouting, "Come on you lot. You're not working hard enough!"

When we were getting ready for one of our matches in the 1974–5 season, Tommy Hughes came up to me and said, "I want you to know that you and I are to throw this game. Money will be left for us both after the game. I'm just letting you know what's happened, but I'm not doing it." There was no way I would take a bribe and, as if I needed confirmation that I'd made the right decision, ten minutes before kick-off, John Sillett stormed into the room. He stood in front of me and roared at the dressing room, "I've just heard that someone has been offered a bribe to throw this match. If I find out that someone has, their feet won't touch the ground. They will be finished."

The drama didn't finish with John's pre-match tirade. During the game I clashed with one of their players in their penalty area and I could tell straight away that I had injured the ligaments in my right knee. I now had a problem. I really needed to go off, as I was in agony. But remembering John's talk I thought, if I go off now, will he think that I am feigning injury and suspect me of being bribed? I also thought, if I don't take this penalty and stay on, what will he think? So I decided to take the penalty. But even as I prepared to take the spot kick, I panicked. What if I miss? Thankfully I scored, and ended up with my leg in plaster which meant I missed the rest of the season. The game ended in a 2–2 draw and when Tommy Hughes came into the dressing room at the end of the game, he looked at me and said, "Thank God for that". I knew exactly what he meant.

We finished the season in twelfth position and would have done better had it not been for our terrible form away from home. We only managed two victories on the road, against Gillingham and Colchester United. At home, we were a very different proposition, winning fourteen and losing only three of our twenty-three games.

Despite the disappointment of finishing in mid table, for me, my first season at Edgar Street was something of a triumph. I finished as top scorer at the club with thirty-two goals, thirty-one of which were in the league. It was also the highest number of goals I had scored in any of my seasons as a professional player. As well as being voted Player of the Season by the fans, I also received the Rothman's Golden Boot for being the highest scorer in all four divisions of the Football League. Although I was honoured to receive such a prize, I have to say that it was a very ordinary looking thing, and not something you would put pride of place on your mantelpiece, it's a plastic plaque.

One of the other incredible things in my first year at Hereford happened in the pre-season. In a match against a Gibraltar XI, I managed to score four goals in a 15–0 victory. The result was the club's highest score and beat the 11–0 FA Cup victory against Thynnes Athletic which had stood since 1947.

The 1975–6 season will never be forgotten by Hereford United fans. It was the year that the club who, just three years earlier, had been playing non-league football in the Southern League, made it to the Second Division of the Football League. What was even more incredible was that we didn't just sneak in, but we went up as champions. Despite that, we didn't make a particularly good start. We only won one of our first five games and for the first half of the season we were never in the top spot. We didn't reach that position until the beginning of February after we demolished Cardiff City (who eventually finished runners up) 4–1 at Edgar Street in front of nearly 13,000 fans. I was thrilled with the score, not just because it put us at the top of the table, but also because the goal I scored after eight minutes was my fiftieth for Hereford United in less than two seasons.

Once we got to pole position we never lost it, and we secured promotion with a goalless draw away to Walsall. One week later, again in front of a 12,000 crowd, we won the derby match against Shrewsbury Town 3–1, to be confirmed as champions.

It is interesting to ask why the team was so much more successful in this than in the previous season. I think it was down to the signings which John Sillett made. The goalkeeper Kevin Charlton came in from Bournemouth to create competition with Tommy Hughes. Steve Davey, the ex-Plymouth Argyle striker, joined me up front and together we scored over fifty goals. John Galley, who had moved to Edgar Street from Nottingham Forest, was a centre forward who could also play at centre half. Steve Ritchie, a left back, from Greenock Morton and midfielder Jimmy Lindsay from Colchester United completed the new signings. Roy Carter, who had played just one game for the Bulls the previous season, having signed from Cornish team Falmouth Town, developed as a player and made over thirty appearances in the Championship-winning side.

Although it was a great season as far as I was concerned, there were a few dark moments. In late September, when as a team we were still struggling to find our form, we beat Swindon Town 1–0 at home, with a goal from Steve Emery. After the game the players were invited to the vice-president's meal. Instead of the event being a celebration of an important victory, in his speech, John Sillett chose the occasion to challenge me about my performance. As far as he was concerned, John felt that I should have scored a hat-trick. His demanding attitude persisted throughout the season and even after we had won the championship, he was still unhappy. After lifting the League trophy in our 3–1 defeat of Shrewsbury Town on Easter Monday, we played Rotherham United the following Saturday, again at home. I scored after two minutes and by half-time we were 3–0 ahead. In the second half, Rotherham came back and reduced the deficit, so that the final score was 3–2. John told us and the press that he was furious about our ill-discipline.

A week after the Swindon match, when, according to John Sillett, I should have scored at least three goals,

I suffered another dark moment in our home match against Gillingham. I jumped in the air to challenge the goalkeeper for a high ball, and he hit me on the back of the head. As I hit the ground, I realised that I couldn't move my right arm or right leg. When Peter Isaacs, the club physio reached me, I said, "Don't touch my neck." About half a minute later everything seemed to come rushing back through my arm and my leg. I had the most awful pins and needles and terrible pain.

At the hospital they put me in a brace which you could inflate to take the neck away from the spine. When I returned to the club John Sillett said, "You can still run, so you might as well do some light training. We'll devise our own treatment for you here at the ground."

The 'devised treatment' consisted of them lifting me up until I was hanging from the goal posts. They would leave me there until I fell off. Once I hit the ground they would pick me up and put me back. This would happen for about thirty minutes. In the period that I was injured, the team won three, drew one and lost one. After three weeks of being out of the team John Sillett told me that I might as well start full training again.

Very early on in my first session, the ball hit my head and also the damaged nerve. I fell on my knees in terrible pain. Within thirty seconds I felt alright, and was able to get up. John came over to me and said, "Carry on, just make sure you don't head the ball." Ten years later I discovered that I had fractured the vertebrae in my neck.

While I was still unable to play in games, but able to train with the boys, the manager came to me and said, "We're playing Peterborough on Saturday. I don't expect you to play but I will name you as the sub." John claimed that he was doing this so that Peterborough United could worry about the prospect of me coming on during the match. When we played the game, we were third in the table and the Posh were ninth.

When the score was level at 1–1, John said, "Warm up. I'm not going to put you on. I just want to frighten them." In the second half we were 1–3 down with fifteen minutes left. Despite all the promises before and during the match, he brought Eric Redrobe off and sent me on instead. It is one thing for your manager to tell you to play in a football match and make sure you don't head the ball. It is a very different matter to be involved in a game and avoid letting the ball have contact with your head. Instinct kicks in and, in the heat of the match, you find yourself doing what you always do. The ball came over and, without thinking, I headed it. What had happened to me in training happened now at London Road. The next thing I remember was being on the ground, on my hands and knees in excruciating pain. I battled on to the end of the match and we lost 2–4.

Despite what had happened at Peterborough, I was in the starting line up at Deepdale the following week. It was a top of the table clash, with us in third position and Preston North End one place below us. The Lillywhites were undefeated in twelve games and the contest proved to be one of the best matches of the season. When I scored in the fifty-seventh minute we were 3–1 ahead. Three minutes later, they reduced the arrears with a penalty, only for Jimmy Lindsay to score a minute later to restore our two goal lead. Two minutes after Jimmy's goal, Preston North End scored again to make the score 4–3 in our favour, which is how it remained until the final whistle. Bobby Charlton was the manager at Deepdale, and it took me ten years to discover that he had made an offer for me after that game. Apparently the Hereford management rejected his £80,000, saying they wanted £100,000 for me.

The match against Preston North End at Edgar Street was also memorable for me. It was the last game of the season and we had already been crowned as Third Division champions. I needed to score two goals to be the highest scorer in all four divisions of the Football League for the second successive season and, of course, to win the rather dull Rothman's Golden Boot again. At half-time, we were trailing 0–1, but in the second half I managed to score a hat-trick to give us a 3–1 victory. In many ways that game was more exciting than the match a few weeks previously, when we had secured promotion with a goalless draw away to Walsall. Although the atmosphere had been terrific, with 2,500 fans making the journey from Hereford to the Midlands, winning promotion that day turned out to be one of the biggest anticlimaxes in my playing career.

I suppose there were a few reasons why I felt slightly flat at the final whistle. With Alan Buckley playing for Walsall and myself on the field, it meant that the two top scorers in the league were playing against each other. Despite that fact, the game ended in a goalless draw. The result was also a reason why I felt slightly down. We had played for a goalless draw, which was not like us. As a team we had scored eighty-six goals in the championship-winning season. The decision to go for a 0–0 draw was not the manager's idea. Before the game, the players decided we would chase everything, give nothing away and close the opposition down. I suppose

I was also slightly miffed that right at the end I missed a sitter. It would have been nice to celebrate gaining promotion by scoring the winning goal.

Despite the slight anticlimax, it was wonderful to be involved in the Hereford United story. I felt I was part of a fairy tale as fans, players and management began to contemplate competing against top teams in the Second Division so soon after playing non-league football. It was incredible to think that a tiny team like the Bulls had achieved so much. Although I scored more goals than in the previous season, with a total of thirty-seven, and I won the Rothman's Golden Boot again, I didn't win the club's Player of the Year award, as I had in 1975. In fact, no individual player won it. While we were all wondering which one of us would win the votes of the fans, the Supporters' Association released a statement in which they explained that, in the furore of winning the League, they had forgotten to distribute the forms. Because of that mistake, they decided to award the Player of the Year to the entire team.

In addition to winning the League, we also reached the Welsh Cup final, after defeating Stourbridge, Newport County, Porthmadog and Shrewsbury in previous rounds. The final turned out to be a total farce. At that time, it was played over two legs, home and away. The first leg at Edgar Street ended 2–2, with Peter Spiring scoring two goals. What happened next was very strange, because our opponents, Cardiff City, did not protest, but the Welsh FA decided there had been some mix up over Spiring's papers. As far as they were concerned he was ineligible to play, so the result was eventually scrapped. The Welsh FA then ruled that the two games had to be played within twenty-four hours of each other. On 18 May at Edgar Street, I gave us a 3–2 lead with fifteen minutes left on the clock, only for Phil Dwyer to equalise in the eighty-seventh minute. In the second leg at Ninian Park, we went down 2–3 to lose the final 5–6 on aggregate.

Due to the fact that the games had been hastily arranged, the attendances were very low. Just a month previously, over 35,000 fans had watched us play Cardiff City at Ninian Park in a top of the table clash. For the second leg, just over 2,000 turned up, and we didn't do much better at Edgar Street with 3,709 watching the 3–3 draw. Many of the fans were away on holiday and others knew nothing about the hastily arranged games. It was not only the fans who struggled with the decision of the Welsh FA, Jimmy Lindsay had to break short his holidays and Terry Paine came back from Calcutta. It was a shame that such a wonderful season had to end in such a ridiculous way.

The 1976–7 season was Hereford United's first in the big time of Division Two. We were the minnow of all minnows. Yet, despite knowing our limitations, we made a great start. The first ever Second Division match at Edgar Street ended with us beating Hull City 1–0. I was chuffed to score the first ever goal for the club at this level, and even happier when it turned out to be the winner. We then drew 1–1 away to Sheffield United and then a 3–0 home victory over Burnley (in which I scored a hat-trick), put us in the heady heights of sixth in the table. I'm afraid that was as good as it got as we then went on a run of ten games without a victory. During that bad run we played Fulham at Craven Cottage. On the way down on the bus, John Sillett came up to me and said, "Do it for us today. They've looked at you and they're worried you can do it against them." George Best had come back from his time playing in America and he was alongside Rodney Marsh. Despite John's hopes, the match failed to be the 'Dixie Show' and turned into the 'Rodney and George Show' instead. They were on a different planet of football skills to the rest of us. I watched most of it from up front. I did touch the ball a couple of times, but if ever I got hold of it, there was then the slight problem of trying to get past the great Bobby Moore. We lost 1–4 and the following week we were thrashed 1–6 at home by Wolverhampton Wanderers. Steve Kindon on the left wing completely murdered us, scoring once and making all the other goals.

In so many of the games we played, we were up against star players. Southampton had Rodrigues, Ted McDougall, Mick Channon and Peter Osgood, yet despite having all that talent in their ranks, they still only managed to finish ninth. It was difficult for us to compete against these great teams. In our final nine games, we lost only once, but that terrible run early in the season cost us our place in the division and we were relegated, despite beating Southampton 2–0 at home. Looking back on that season, perhaps we had overachieved the season before. Once we were in the Second Division we hit a brick wall. We ran out of revenue and couldn't afford the great players we needed to stay up in that division.

At the end of the season John Sillett called me into the office and said, "I'm going to get the sack. I've had an offer for you from Wrexham. They will pay £60,000. They will get what they want, and you will get what you want, which is promotion, they are the best side in their league."

John was like a second dad to me, strict but fair. After every game he would cry "Only two?" He always wanted me to get a hat-trick. He was a top man for me.

5

Changing from
a Bull into a Robin

ALTHOUGH JOHN SILLETT was very enthusiastic about my move to Wrexham, predicting that I would help them into the Second Division, I have to admit that, at first, I didn't share his excitement. In fact, when I told Dana that a move to the Welsh town was on the cards, her first response was to say, "Where is it?" Unfortunately, being born and bred in Leicestershire, I couldn't really help. I had only been to the country once and that was to stay at a B&B on the West Promenade in Llandudno with my parents and Dana, when I was seventeen years old.

It was arranged that we should go for talks with Arfon Griffiths, the manager, and the club secretary, Norman Wilson. Dana and I drove there and, in the late 1970s, the town was in a bad way. Before the recent redevelopment, it looked run down and sorry for itself. Not really knowing the best way into the town, we entered via Marchweil along the Kings Mill Road. Over to our right, we were welcomed to our potential new home by the derelict Rubery Owen factory. Approaching the football ground along the Mold Road was even worse. The first sight was the dilapidated-looking Supporters' Association hut. Behind that we could see corrugated sheets and at the rear of those the wall near the Kop was covered in barbed wire. Once we drove down Crispin Road and into the main car park behind the Yale Stand, it was a different world. Wow! was the reaction from both of us. After we spoke for a while, Norman and Arfon invited us both to lunch at the Pant yr Ochain Hotel. It was the first time in my football career that I had been courted like this.

Arfon had taken over the club from John Neal after the team had narrowly missed out on promotion the previous season. The fans had endured the agony of seeing promotion snatched away from them in the last few minutes of the penultimate game of the season, against Crystal Palace. At 2–2 with just five minutes to go, Wrexham were on their way to the Second Division for the first time in their history. Then, Palace struck twice to win 4–2, and it meant that Wrexham needed to beat Mansfield in the final game, but they drew 0–0.

That narrow failure had left a cloud over the Racecourse, which had deepened when manager John Neal accepted an invitation to manage First Division Middlesborough. I knew that if I joined the club I would have a large hole to fill. The number nine shirt had been worn by Billy Ashcroft who, as well as being a prolific goal scorer, had also been the fans' favourite. He had also followed Neal to Middlesborough. Even to this day, if I see him at an event, Billy Ashcroft will sneak up behind me, tap me on the shoulder and say, "Come on then who was the best centre forward Wrexham ever had?" He's such a big fellow and I never argue with him!

Wrexham made a poor start in their first seven games of the new season. They collected only five points with one win, three draws and three defeats. In the summer Arfon had signed two players from the First Division, John Roberts from Birmingham City and Les Cartwright from Coventry City. He'd obviously hoped that their vast experience, combined with the youthfulness of players such as Mickey Thomas and Alan Hill, would give him the missing ingredient for promotion. It obviously wasn't working and, in the week he interviewed me, he also signed the international goalkeeper, Dai Davies, from First Division Everton.

At the end of our day at the Racecourse, I think Arfon and Norman were shocked when I said that I needed twenty-four hours to consider their offer. This is something I have always done throughout my football career, as it is important to consider any potential move from the viewpoint of my family.

The following day, a Wednesday, I became a Wrexham player and was almost immediately nobbled by Dave Lovett of the *Wrexham Evening Leader* newspaper. He looked me straight in the eye and said, "Don't you think that £60,000 is an awful lot of money to pay for a thirty-year-old footballer?" Welcome to Wrexham, I thought to myself, and thanks a lot Dave. Mercifully, since that first day as a Wrexham player, Dave Lovett has become a very close friend.

After two days of training with my new team mates, I began to realise that the club had some very skilful players: Les Cartwright, John Roberts, Dai Davies were all internationals who had played at the highest level, while Mickey Thomas was to go on and become a

Manchester United star and Bobby Shinton would sign for First Division Manchester City.

Having signed midweek, I had little time to settle in before my debut, which was against Swindon Town at the Racecourse. I managed to settle my nerves by scoring after sixteen minutes. Mickey Thomas screamed down the left wing, crossed the ball and I managed to hit it first time. I connected well and the ball ended up in the back of the net – but I did have a bit of luck, because it went through the goalie's legs. All the reports said I scored from seven yards, but I would like to make that eight, as it sounds much better! Although in many ways seven yards from the goal line is always the scorer's domain and, as a poacher of goals, I've made this my area.

When the goal went in I could not believe the noise the crowd made. Bobby Shinton ran up to me, put his arm around me and said, "Come on, let's celebrate with the fans." He took me over to the packed Yale Stand, and I enjoyed the adulation of the Wrexham fans for the first time in my life. In earlier times, I had rarely celebrated the scoring of a goal, but Shinton taught me to milk it for all it was worth. I must confess that when he suggested running across the pitch, I was a little nervous as a thirty-year-old striker should conserve his energy!

Later in the game Graham Whittle scored to give us a 2–0 lead and, although Swindon pulled a goal back in the last twenty minutes, we held on to win 2–1. At the end of the game I was delighted to have started my new career with a goal. I also realised how nervous I had been before kick-off, with so much to live up to. Not only was I stepping into Ashcroft's boots, but I also had a record of scoring one goal in every two games to maintain. A new defender at a club is given time to bed in, but a striker is expected to score all the time.

The victory over Swindon was the start of an unbeaten run of thirteen games. This included a visit to my old club, Exeter City, in October. This was a club that I felt had let me down and released me after I'd finished as their top scorer. I had a lot to prove to their fans and management. Unfortunately, we hardly got a kick in the match, as Exeter played us off the park but, as we went into the final minutes, we were still drawing 0–0. In the final minute of the game, Bobby Shinton crossed the ball, I rose above the Exeter defence and headed in the winner. I said earlier that I rarely celebrated my goals, but on this occasion I went absolutely wild. Although it is unlikely that any of the directors who had got rid of me were still at the club, I was still overcome with joy. Dave Lovett's headline the following evening was 'Wrexham's Floodlight Robbery at St James' Park', but I didn't care!

Three weeks later, after defeating Bury 3–1 at the Racecourse, we moved to the top spot in the table. As the result of the disappointment of the previous season, one or two players, such as Gareth Davies, feared that we had peaked too soon. However, there was a great atmosphere in the dressing room and a buzz on the terraces. In early December 1977, I had another opportunity to face one of my old clubs. Hereford United were the visitors, and we won 2–1 with goals from Graham Whittle and Les Cartwright. At the end of the game Arfon came into the dressing room and asked me in a very worried tone if I was alright. It's the only time in my career that a manager has shown such concern for my well-being, and it was because I had been kicked off the park by the Hereford team. I discovered afterwards that my dear friend John Sillett, who was still Hereford's manager, had given a team talk in which he had said, "Don't let McNeil get the ball, but if he does, kick him off the park." After the match John Sillett turned to me and said with a huge grin, "You won't ever score a goal against one of my teams." The Hereford goal was scored by Kevin Sheedy who, of course, was to become a major Everton star. Interestingly, his goal was the first Hereford had scored away from home since early season, when I had scored in my last game for Hereford, away to Chesterfield. I had not wanted to play in that game as I had injured my abductor muscle. When I told John that I was injured he said, "You've got to play, Wrexham have got people here tonight to watch you." It meant that when I signed for the Reds, I was still nursing an injury, but Arfon and the medical staff decided it was minor and that I would soon recover full fitness.

Around the time of the Hereford game I was beginning to wonder if I had made a mistake in moving to Wrexham. After nine weeks at the club I had only scored five goals. Having tasted promotion twice with the Bulls, I had come to Wrexham for only one thing, and that was to take them into the Second Division. I didn't feel I was playing as well as I should.

My main problem was that I found it difficult to play with Bobby Shinton and Graham Whittle. The trouble with Bobby was that I never knew when or if he was going to cross the ball. He was a great ball player and he would tear down the wing past a defender, and so I would start my run into the box. Unfortunately, he would then check and beat another player. In the meantime, I was in no-man's-land waiting for a ball that never came. Bobby was a great favourite with the crowd, and sometimes he would enjoy their chants of "Ole" so much that he would go back and beat another player. It took me a long time to realise that he would not cross until the third or fourth time. Although Graham Whittle was not on the wing, he was similar to Bobby and he would often have one or two more touches on the ball than I was expecting. And of course it wasn't just Bobby and Graham who gave me these problems. I had similar difficulties with Noddy (Mickey Thomas). All three were great individual ball players and tended to work on their own. It took me some time to figure how to best manage my own runs. I know that I am ultra-competitive when it comes to a football game, and the frustration of not feeling that I was scoring as many goals as I should have led to my early uncertainty at the club.

A week after the Hereford game, we were at Valley Parade playing against Bradford City. I scored from a header at the start of the second half and, with just two minutes remaining, it looked as if my goal would win us the game. It would also have meant we were undefeated in the league for fourteen games and we'd have equalled the club record of eighteen league and Cup games without defeat. Then, in the eighty-eighth minute, disaster struck. Gareth Davies scored an own goal and a minute later Bradford scored through Hutchins to win 2–1.

Despite the disappointment of losing our unbeaten run, we managed to go another seven games without defeat, until we lost 1–2 away to Oxford on 3 March. Of course our league form was punctuated by great Cup runs in the League and FA Cups. Unfortunately, because

I was Cup tied, I couldn't play in the League Cup, but the boys had knocked out First Division Bristol City and Second Division Charlton Athletic on their way to a home quarter-final tie against Liverpool, which we lost 1–3, with Kenny Dalglish scoring a hat-trick. Bill Shankley described our team as the best outside the First Division and throughout the season he would often watch us at midweek games and pop into the dressing room to wish us well.

When I scored one of the goals against non-league Burton Albion in our FA Cup first round 2–0 home win, I had no idea that I was embarking on a record which still stands to this day. Over the next three seasons, I was to score in ten successive rounds. After Burton, we defeated Preston 2–0 and I scored one of the goals, while Gareth Davies got the other. This victory gave us a third round encounter against First Division Bristol City, who we had already dumped out of the League Cup. Trailing 0–2 we stormed back to lead 4–2, but then conceded two late goals in the last seven minutes. In the replay at the Racecourse, in front of 15,000 raucous fans, we won 3–0. Defeating Bristol City meant that we had an away tie against Newcastle, which we drew 2–2. Playing in front of the *Match of the Day* cameras, we fell behind to a John Bird goal in the fifty-sixth minute, but two minutes later, I equalised. In the sixty-fifth minute, Ray Blackhall miss hit a shot which flew past Dai Davies in goal, to give Newcastle the lead. They held it until the last minute, when I managed to volley in the equaliser to level the tie at 2–2. In the replay, in front of 18,000 fans, we outplayed our First Division opponents and hammered them 4–1. Bobby Shinton and Les Cartwright scored and I got the other two.

In the fifth round we had a home tie against fellow giant killers Blyth Spartans. The side from the north-east had already put out First Division Stoke. On a rock hard pitch on a bitterly cold February afternoon, we struggled to break down the non-leaguers. Before the game we had all agonised about what footwear to use. Some of the lads played in all-weather pumps, which had grip for frosty conditions. I opted for studs and was to regret the decision later in the game. In one tackle I landed badly on my heel, and tore the facia tendon in my foot. Blyth took the lead after twelve minutes, following a back pass by Alan Hill which Terry Johnson intercepted before scoring. With a minute to go, we were still trailing and were awarded a corner. The Blyth players and fans were adamant that it was not a corner. Their view seemed to be shared by the *Match of the Day* cameramen and pundits. To add insult to injury, the referee allowed Les Cartwright to take it three times because the flag kept falling over. The Blyth goalkeeper caught the ball from the first two only to have to face a third attempt. It was this one which beat everyone in the goal area, but fell for me, and I scored at the far post.

Blyth decided that their ground was too small for the replay, and they switched the match to Newcastle's ground at St James' Park. When our team bus pulled up outside the ground, we couldn't believe how few people were there waiting to get in. We all assumed that we'd be playing in a near-empty stadium. When we got onto the pitch to warm up, we couldn't believe our eyes. The ground was packed to the rafters. The Kop was a sea of green and white scarves (the Blyth colours). The match was a sell-out and those people who we had seen outside the ground were obviously the unlucky ones who couldn't get in to see the game. The crowd was 42,264, a record attendance for a non-league club, which stood until 2011, when over 70,000 watched Crawley Town lose 0–1 against Manchester United at Old Trafford.

Just as they had done at the Racecourse, Blyth gave us a hard game in the replay. After eight minutes I got into the Blyth penalty area and their centre half, Tom Dixon, pushed me in the back. As I had won the spot kick, I assumed that I should take it, so I was slightly annoyed when Graham Whittle picked the ball up and moved towards the spot as if he was going to take it.

"Give me the ball," I said.

"No, you're not going to take it."

"You'd better score," I shouted, or words to that effect.

"Why do you want to take it anyway? You're bound to score, some time in the game," Whittle replied.

So I stood at the edge of the box and very grumpily watched Graham score from the spot and put us 1–0 ahead. I think there was a bit of anger in his shot too, as he didn't place the ball but just lambasted it into the net.

Strangely, about twenty minutes later, Graham's prediction came true. Blyth had a free kick at our end of the pitch and they knocked the ball into our goal area. We cleared our lines to the right hand side of the pitch, where it was picked up by Bobby Shinton. As I saw Shinton control the ball, I ran through the middle. The conditions were perfect for me as they would have been for a horse – plenty of mud. Eventually Bobby crossed, I steadied myself and hit it on the half volley. The ball went from the top left corner of the net into the left hand side of the goal. I have never scored a goal in such eerie circumstances. The whole stadium and 43,000 people fell silent.

Later in the game, Dai Davies tried to retrieve the ball and during a goal mouth scramble, he was kicked in the hand.

I ran up to him and asked, "Are you OK?"

"No, not really," said Dai. "Don't tell anyone, but I've broken my hand." Dai battled on to the end of the game, which we won 2–1. That was the last game he played for us that season and his place was taken between the posts by Eddie Niedzwiecki. Very shortly, I was to join Dai on the injury list.

In that first game against Blyth Spartans at the Racecourse, the pitch had been rock hard and during the game I fell badly and, as already mentioned, I tore the facia tendon in my foot, which was incredibly painful. The only reason I was able to play in the replay at Newcastle was because the physio had given me five cortisone injections in five days.

I managed to play three more games in the league. My last league appearance was at home to my old club Exeter City on 4 March. With two minutes to go, we were drawing 1–1 and then I managed to score the winner. As always, it was like a dream come true to put one over on a side that had let me go.

The following week we were drawn at home to Arsenal in the quarter-finals of the FA Cup. Despite my injury, I was desperate to play and pleaded with Arfon Griffiths and George Showell to allow me to take to the field. As the cortisone injections were no longer working, in desperation, I went to Chester to see an acupuncturist.

It worked, and I played for the full ninety minutes in a game which we lost 2–3, but according to Terry Neill, the Gunners' manager, and the *Match of the Day* pundits, we should have won. The next day I was in total agony and couldn't move because of the pain in my foot.

It meant that I missed the rest of the season and watched our run in to the Championship from the stands. It was an incredibly frustrating time. As a striker, I wouldn't care if a defender scored, but I didn't want any of the strikers to bag any goals. Don't believe players who say they don't care who scores. For two seasons at Hereford I had scored thirty-five and thirty-seven goals respectively. In this, my first season at Wrexham, I was keen to finish as top scorer. It was murder to watch from the stands, as the boys scored six against Tranmere Rovers at home and four against Carlisle United away. In the end, I finished with the highest number of goals, but only just. My tally of twenty-four was followed by Graham Whittle on twenty-three and Bobby Shinton on twenty-two.

Despite many resounding wins and good unbeaten runs, we finished the season with only one win from our last ten games. But what a win that was. We needed to beat Rotherham to be assured of promotion to the Second Division for the first time in our history. We were 5–0 up at half-time, and we went on to win 7–1. There were great scenes at the end of the game, with the fans pouring onto the field to celebrate something which had never been achieved before in the club's fifty-seven year Football League history. I even managed to hobble onto the pitch with the help of my crutches. It was great to be caught up in the atmosphere, but I would have preferred to have been playing. When we won promotion at Hereford, the fans had been all around us, and it was magical to be out on the pitch when the final whistle blew.

Having only played twenty-three games I felt slightly disappointed although, when I went on the open-top bus ride around the town, I realised what we had achieved and how much it meant to the fans. My goals had obviously helped, and now I had to get fit and look forward to the next season.

6

The Big Time

THE 19TH OF August 1978 was a historic day for the town of Wrexham. For the first time in its history the football club was to play host to a Second Division fixture. Over 14,000 fans turned up at the Racecourse to see the Robins take on Brighton and Hove Albion. However, what should have been a memorable and exciting day was spoiled by the game – it was the most boring match I have ever seen in my life.

In the previous season we had built up a reputation as an attacking team that scored goals for fun. The Seagulls came for a point, and decided to 'park their bus in front of their goal'. It was impossible to break them down and their negative tactics frustrated us as players. The crowd also grew unhappy and booed and slow handclapped the visitors.

I suppose you could say there were two positives to be taken from the match. Firstly, we learned as a team that life in the second tier would be harder than the one we had enjoyed the year before. We would have to work very hard to break teams down. Secondly, I was pleased to renew contact with and play against Mark

Lawrenson, these days a *Match of the Day* pundit. As a forward you build up relationships over the years with some of the defenders who mark you. I certainly did this with Lawro and enjoyed our battles in games against Brighton, Preston and Peterborough. He certainly had an outstanding game that day.

We made a fairly good start to the season and, after six games, were undefeated and in third position, having won two and drawn four. The only problem was that three of those draws were at home and had all ended goalless, with our blank against Brighton being followed by the same score in games against Leicester City and Newcastle United. This meant that by the time we played Cardiff City at the Racecourse on the last day of September, the fans had still not seen a goal. On that day we solved the problem, with John Lyons gaining the distinction of scoring the first Second Division home goal for the club and, of course, the first ever Second Division goal at the Racecourse. Unfortunately for him, the fans and the players, Cardiff scored more and returned to south Wales as 2–1 victors.

One of the main reasons I had been attracted to join Wrexham was their fantastic Cup record and the fact that, as regular winners of the Welsh Cup, they had qualified on several occasions to play in Europe. We were drawn against the Yugoslavian Cup winners, and in September we made the journey to play Rijeka. Their ground is one of the most amazing I have ever played at. It seemed to be hewn out of a large rock and many of the fans watched the game a hundred feet up, sitting on the rocks with their legs dangling in the air.

We were 0–2 down at half-time and I have to admit

that I gave away a silly free kick on the half way line. It was one of those situations: one ball into the penalty area, one header and one goal. At half-time Arfon blamed me for the goal. I replied, "When he took the free kick there were eleven bloody defenders in front of him weren't there? So why didn't they do something?"

I don't think the boss was too impressed by my sense of humour and ten minutes into the second half, he took me off. Whenever Arfon and I meet up now, which is pretty regular, we always have a laugh about it. At the time I felt a bit miffed, and went back to the hotel and sank a few glasses of wine. We were well and truly beaten 0–3, and Arfon reckoned they were the best side Wrexham had ever met in Europe.

Although the tie seemed to be dead, 10,000 fans turned up for the second leg at the Racecourse. They made a fantastic racket and really got behind us. Ten minutes into the second half, Mel Sutton sent over a fantastic cross. I managed to hit it on the turn and score. Ten minutes later, Les Cartwright banged in number two and with twenty-five minutes still left, the game really started to feel as if we could turn the disaster in Yugoslavia into another famous victory. Looking back, I feel I should have scored more than one, as I had quite a few chances. Despite the fantastic atmosphere the fans created and the great effort of the team, it wasn't to be.

In November of that season my son Jamie was born, and as he grew up he became a Wrexham fan, and was later an apprentice at the football club under Brian Flynn. Although released by them, he has remained a stalwart supporter of the club, is a season ticket holder and watches them with my grandchildren Jack, 7 and

Morgan, 4, both of whom also love playing football – and who knows, they may play the game professionally too.

Having been dumped out of Europe at the first attempt and the League Cup in the second round to Norwich, our hopes for Cup glory turned to the FA Cup. In the third round we were drawn at home to Fourth Division Stockport County. Because of a spell of arctic weather, the match was called off nine times. The weather conditions were so bad that, before the game, the ball and the players' boots had to be dipped in meths so that the snow wouldn't stick to them. When the game finally got under way, the playing surface was covered in two inches of snow. We won 6–2 and I scored a hat-trick. After the game many people talked about one of my goals as if it was the best I had ever scored for Wrexham. I can remember jumping for a brilliant cross from Steve Fox and I felt as if I were suspended in midair for ever. The header went into the top corner and I suppose it must have looked from the terraces as if it were a superb goal. The truth of the matter is that, by the time I got up in the air, I couldn't see a thing because the sun was in my eyes, and the ball hit me on the forehead before finding its own way into the back of the net. Still, I'm quite happy to claim it as a brilliant goal!

For me, the highlight of the season came in the next round, when we were drawn away to Tottenham Hotspur. They had a star-studded side, with the likes of Glen Hoddle, Ricky Villa and Ossie Ardilles in the team. I had watched these players on television and had admired their skill. For me Hoddle always seemed to glide along the pitch and he was a great passer of the ball, with loads of pace. The atmosphere at White Hart Lane was sensational with 27,000 watching the game. At one stage of the match, we were trailing 1–2, but then we came back into it and, with eight minutes left, we were leading 3–2. It was starting to look as if we would repeat what Wrexham had done in 1976 in the League Cup, when they had won by the same scoreline at the same ground. Unfortunately, Chris Jones popped up to head the equaliser for a 3–3 draw. In the replay in front of a 16,000 crowd, Gareth Davies managed to cancel out Jones' early goal and take the tie into extra time. I scored after eight minutes and we really thought we were going to take another huge scalp. But, it was that man Chris Jones again who undid us, with two late goals to complete his hat-trick and take his tally in the two games to four goals. It was strange how one of the Spurs' Reserves had done so much damage. Perhaps we were too busy trying to stop the star players play.

The terrible weather which had caused us so many problems in our tie against Stockport County also disrupted our league programme. Little did we realise when we lost 1–2 at Deepdale to Preston North End on Boxing Day, that we would not play another league match for two months. During that frosty snap, I took part in the coldest game I have ever experienced. Away to Newcastle at St James' Park, we arrived at the ground to be welcomed by torrential rain, with a howling gale blowing the rain to the far end of the ground. When we started the game there was a lot of surface water on the pitch. Dai Davies in goal, would kick upfield and the ball would stall in the sky and then return to within twenty yards of his goal. It was just as bad for the outfield players, and if you tried to pass to one of your team mates, the ball wouldn't go any further than ten yards. John Roberts, in defence, always insisted on playing in short-sleeved tops, but I think even he regretted the decision that day. The Wrexham players wanted the game to be abandoned, but the referee refused to call it off. Then, when Newcastle scored, they were keen for the game to continue. Just before half-time we equalised and, as we trudged off, the referee told us that the match was being abandoned. Once in the dressing rooms, we took our boots off and dived into a hot bath with all our football kit on. Once out of the bath, I saw one of their players being carried into the boiler room. It was Terry Hibbert. He couldn't stop shivering as he was obviously suffering from hypothermia.

When we lost our first game to the bad weather we were ninth in the league. By the time we played again, an away game to Cambridge on 28 February, we were seventeenth, just a few places above the relegation zone. When we came into the Second Division, many of us in the team believed we could go all the way into the top flight. There was a great camaraderie in the dressing room and, despite the departure of Mickey Thomas to Manchester United in November, Arfon had made some great signings. In October, Joey Jones returned from Liverpool for a club record fee of £210,000. Joey was a brilliant player, who had performed at the highest level with Liverpool, and I think that the fee we paid for him was an absolute steal. Even to this day, if I go out with Joey, I always walk with a limp. If people ask me why I am moving like that, I explain to them that whenever Joey passed the ball to me, I would always have to go up the terraces to retrieve the ball, walking with one leg higher than the other, and that left me with a limp!

Arfon also signed midfielders Steve Fox from Birmingham and Dave Giles from Cardiff. Despite having a good team, by the time we came to play again in late February, the gap was too big for us to catch up. We were always five or six games behind the other teams and, with a small squad and a number of injuries, plus the fact that towards the end of the season we were often playing three or four games in a week, it became an impossible task and we finished the season in fifteenth position.

As well as being great players, Steve Fox and Dave Giles were tremendous characters. When they first signed for the club they stayed at the Crest Hotel in Wrexham. One evening, Arfon Griffiths had a phone call from the management of the hotel, saying there had been a disturbance in one of their rooms. Arfon arrived to discover that they had placed a picture on the back of the door and, in turns, were taking shots at it with an air rifle.

Later in the season Fox and Giles went to Chester and bought an inflatable boat. It was enormous, easily as large as the dinghies used by the Lifeboat service. On their maiden voyage, they pulled the rip cord on the outboard motor, turned up the throttle and went hurtling down the Chester canal straight into a bridge.

By this time they had left the Crest Hotel, and were staying with a Mrs D who put up numerous Wrexham players over the years. As they had decided that the engine was far too powerful, they filled a dustbin with water and placed the engine inside. They thought this would give them more control over the machine and that they'd be able to run it in like a car engine. So they pulled the rip cord and the bin charged down the garden at tremendous speed before smashing into Mrs D's fence. Mrs D was not too pleased with them but I have to say that the fans were pretty impressed with them on the pitch. They were both very skilful players and great crowd pleasers.

They both played in, perhaps, the most controversial game of the season. At Upton Park, away to West Ham, the *Match of the Day* cameras were present to witness an incident that was talked about for a very long time after the final whistle. After twenty-eight minutes the Hammers' striker, Bryan 'Pop' Robson, flicked on a cross with his hand to Billy Bonds, who scored. The referee, Ken Baker, somehow missed the blatant hand ball and awarded the goal. Dai Davies, who didn't normally overreact to situations, was so incensed that he ran down the pitch, chasing the referee. I ran after Dai to try to calm him down. When I reached Dai, he turned round and told me to bugger off. He then grabbed hold of Mr Baker and was promptly sent off. With an hour of the game still left to play, we were down to ten men. We didn't have a substitute goalkeeper, so we started asking around the team to see if anyone fancied going between the posts. We were all slightly taken aback when Wayne Cegielski volunteered, as none of us had ever seen him play in that position. He had an absolute blinder and kept the score down to 1–0 and then, with only two minutes left, we equalised through Bobby Shinton and earned a 1–1 draw. In the dressing room after the game we all told him that we were happy for him to change position, as he was no good where he normally played! We were only joking of course. After he saw a replay of the incident, the referee admitted that he had got it wrong and Pop Robson said that he was not proud of what he'd done, although I'm not sure if I believe him.

So our first eventful season in the Second Division came to an end. We were left wondering what would have happened if the weather hadn't been so unkind to us. Our home form of ten wins and six draws was as good as Stoke's, who were promoted into the top division. It was our away form which let us down, collecting only two wins on the road, both by the same score of 1–0 at Fulham and Leyton Orient. Remarkably, both those wins came in our first week in the division, and for the rest of the season we failed to win away from the Racecourse.

At the beginning of our second season in the Second Division (1979–80) much of the talk was about departures. Bobby Shinton became the first Wrexham player to make use of the new freedom of contract ruling and signed for First Division Manchester City. The other departure, before the season started, saw John Lyons move to Millwall. John had become unsettled at the club, claiming that he had taken a lot of stick from certain sections of the crowd. I felt sorry for John and some of the other local players at the club like Steve Buxton, Neil Salathiel and Peter Williams. In those days, fans seemed to prefer players who came in from other clubs. It was very different to the situation we're now in where, with so many foreign players at the big clubs, fans actually like having local players in the squad. I was always aware when I was playing that John Lyons and some of the other local players got terrible treatment from the terraces. They would be howled and shouted at and sometimes even abused when they went about their business in the town.

Arfon bought Mick Vinter from Notts County to replace Bobby Shinton. The early season was marked by exits from the League Cup and the European Cup

Winners' Cup. After defeating Carlisle in the first round, we were drawn away to First Division Southampton in the second round. The legendary ex-Gunner, Charlie George was their striker and they hammered us 5–0. They outplayed us so much – it felt as if we didn't get a kick throughout the match. Arfon was furious and he told the press, "I'm ashamed and embarrassed to be manager of a side that played as badly as we did. If they play like that again – I won't be manager. This was the poorest performance since I became manager, there is no excuse." As players, we were bitterly disappointed. Given the club's history as giant killers, we fancied our chances on our journey down to the Dell. Of course it wasn't to be and in the second leg at the Racecourse, Southampton really rubbed in their superiority by beating us 0–3, so that we lost the tie on an aggregate of 0–8.

In Europe we were also drawn against formidable opposition. The East German Cup winners, IFC Magdeburg, had won the European Cup Winners' Cup five years earlier when they defeated AC Milan 2–0 in the final. The team they brought to the Racecourse for the first leg contained four full internationals and seven under-23 internationals. In the first minute I managed to head Dave Giles' corner kick into the net to put us ahead. By half-time, the class of the East Germans was beginning to show and we went into the dressing room trailing 1–2. We stormed back in the second half and, through goals from Steve Fox and Steve Buxton, we gained a fantastic victory with a 3–2 win.

Our trip to East Germany for the replay gave me my first taste of Checkpoint Charlie, the border-crossing between East and West Berlin. It was very different from being in Wrexham, and slightly scary. The guards held us there for over an hour while they searched the bus from top to bottom. I'm not sure what they were expecting to find. I don't know if they were acting on behalf of their football club in case we had an extra player smuggled away!

In front of a capacity crowd of 22,000, we battled brilliantly. Mick Vinter put us ahead in the twenty-third minute, but they equalised through Hoffmann and then five minutes later we recovered the lead with a goal from Alan Hill. Against everyone's expectations we went into the dressing room at half-time, leading 2–1.

Early in the second half, their striker Hoffmann popped up again to level the scores at 2–2. It was the fifty-sixth minute when that goal went in and, at that moment, because of our victory at the Racecourse, we were ahead and on our way to the next round. It stayed that way until, with just one minute of normal time left on the clock, Alan Dwyer got hold of the ball and all he had to do was kick for touch and play for time and we would have gone through. But he dilly-dallied, got pressurised by their team and then miss hit a pass which they intercepted and their midfielder Mewes scored. That meant that, with both sides having won 3–2 at home, the scores were level and we headed for extra time. In that added half an hour, we conceded two goals and lost the tie 5–7 on aggregate.

So, we missed the chance of playing Arsenal in the next round, who disposed of Magdeburg 4–3 on aggregate. After the game, in the dressing room we felt that, against one of Europe's top teams, we hadn't so much been beaten but lost the match ourselves. It is incredible to score five goals over two games and still lose. In spite of everything, we felt we could hold our heads up high.

During that season of 1979–80, despite the disaster against top flight Southampton, we gave some of our better performances in the Cup. In the third round we were drawn at home to Charlton Athletic. Ahead by one goal at the interval, there was no real hint of what was to come in the second half. For the last forty-five minutes, we ran riot. Mick Vinter scored a hat-trick and I got two to add to Ian Edwards' goal in the first half, so that we won 6–0.

After drawing with Carlisle United at Brunton Park, we beat them 3–1 at home with Joey Jones getting one to add to my two goals. That win set us up for a mouth-watering tie at Goodison Park against Everton in the fifth round of the FA Cup. Amongst a massive crowd of 44,000 were 15,000 Wrexham fans who had made the short journey across Offa's Dyke to cheer us on. Again, as players, we really fancied our chances, but it was not to be. After the battling spirit of Magdeburg, we let ourselves down and didn't do ourselves justice, losing 2–5.

As well as the disappointment of the players and the fans, there was also a personal disappointment for me. That game brought to an end the fact that I had scored in ten consecutive rounds of the FA Cup. It all started in my first season at the Racecourse, that unforgettable championship winning year. To recap, in the first round I scored one in our 2–0 victory over non-league Burton Albion. In the second round, away to Preston North End, I scored in the very last minute to add to Gareth

Davies' first half goal, to give us a 2–0 win. The next round produced the two remarkable games against First Division Bristol City, in which we drew 4–4 at Ashton Gate followed by a 3–0 success at the Racecourse. I scored in both games. It was First Division opposition again in the fourth round with a visit to St James' Park to take on Newcastle United. In front of the *Match of the Day* cameras, we were a minute away from going out of the Cup when I volleyed the equaliser in the eighty-ninth minute. In the replay I opened the scoring in the second minute and we went on to get a famous giant killing result with a 4–1 victory over the team from the top division. The next round gave us another home battle against a non-league team, when Blyth Spartans visited the Racecourse. And as already mentioned, I equalised with a controversial goal in the last minute. I again scored in the replay at St James' Park and managed a goal in our 2–3 home defeat against Arsenal in the quarter-final at the Racecourse.

I kept the record going in the next season, 1978–9, our first in the Second Division. I scored twice in our third round destruction of Stockport County and once in our replay defeat in the fourth round at home against Tottenham Hotspur. In the next season, after goals against Charlton Athletic and Carlisle United, my record came to an end in that game at Goodison Park.

In that second season in the Second Division 1979–80, I managed a total of twenty goals, fourteen of which were scored in the league, and I finished as top scorer at the club, two ahead of Mick Vinter. It was a relief for me and no doubt to the fans and everyone else connected with the club. A season earlier, I had finished with one of my lowest hauls, scoring just nine goals, with only four goals in the league. Arfon's signing of Welsh international striker Ian Edwards in early November made a huge difference in terms of my ability to score goals. Wrexham paid the then Third Division Chester City £100,000, which was a record fee for the Sealand Road outfit.

In my footballing career I was always one of the shortest attackers (in stature) in the league. Ian was a tall centre forward, strong on the ball and powerful in the air. Before his arrival, because of my goal scoring record, I think a lot of teams had the mentality, 'Stop Dixie from scoring and we'll be alright'. With the new arrival, they now had two players to worry about up front. It meant that I often had more freedom to get into good positions while they were marking Ian. Also, when he won good ball in the air, I was able to feed off his crumbs.

Just a few weeks after Arfon signed Ian, I scored arguably one of my greatest goals. It was at home against Chelsea in front of a crowd of 15,000. Berrota, one of the first foreign keepers to ply his trade in England, was in goal for the Pensioners and the *Match of the Day* cameras were recording the game. A cross came in from the right and I collected the ball with my right foot, which has always been my weakest. In the split second that I had to work things out, I realised that if I hit it with my favoured left foot, the ball would go miles wide. So I took a chance, and hit it with my right. To this day I can still see Berrota diving, trying to prevent the ball curling into the bottom right hand corner of his net. All my team mates were killing themselves laughing because they knew that I was normally not so good with my right foot. The goal was one of the ten that were selected for December's Goal of the Month competition on *Match of the Day* and whilst lots of people might argue that it wasn't the best goal I ever scored, it was definitely the best right footer.

As well as setting a new club record of scoring in ten consecutive FA Cup rounds, I set another record that season which still stands. On 13 October 1979 I scored the only goal in our 1–0 defeat of Birmingham City at the Racecourse. That goal started a sequence which lasted until our 1–0 home victory over Newcastle on 9 February 1980. During those four months, I scored in eleven consecutive home League and Cup matches. That run featured some interesting home games, such as our 1–0 win over Swansea City. Steve Fox set me up with a beautiful pass and, from the edge of the box, I scored with a full-blooded left footer. John Toshack, the Swans manager said after the game that he was disappointed to lose, but he praised my goal. The other interesting fact about that game is that Dave Giles had been sold to the south Wales club a few days before the match, and he was making his debut for them. Two weeks later, our 3–1 victory over Luton Town saw me make my first appearance in midfield for Wrexham, and I marked the occasion by scoring the first goal in the fifteenth minute. Also during that record, we beat Preston North End in a New Year's Day fixture and their manager, the legendary Nobby Styles, paid us the compliment of saying that Wrexham were the best team he had seen all season.

When I look back on that season I realise that we were competing up near the top for a great part of the campaign. At the beginning of March, with eleven games to go, we were in ninth position. But those last few games proved to be our undoing and we only managed two wins. That saw us finish the season in sixteenth place, but I honestly believe we were a better side than the position suggests and we produced some great performances against top sides.

Although we didn't have as many games cancelled as the previous season, we still lost quite a few games to the weather. Somehow we always seemed to be playing catch up. There were times when the playing schedule was punishing, if not mad. Over Easter we played three games in four days, a Good Friday 1–0 victory over Burnley at home, a 0–0 draw at Preston the following day, with a 0–1 defeat to Sunderland, back at the Racecourse, on Easter Monday. And the modern-day footballers complain about the pressures of the game!

Our small squad and the fact that we suffered lots of injuries also didn't help. With thirteen wins and two draws, our home form was as good as some of the teams in the top five but, yet again, we were let down by our performances away from home, with only three wins. Although disappointed with our final position, I was honoured to be voted Player of the Season by the fans and pleased to get my scoring back on track.

7

Struggling to hold on

AFTER THE EUPHORIA of winning the Third Division Championship and enjoying two years in the higher division, the 1980–1 season was a huge struggle. In the two previous seasons we had always been high up for most of the campaign and then slipped towards the end of the year into the bottom half. This time it was completely different. From the end of October we were in the bottom half and stayed there for the rest of the season, only securing our status as a Second Division side with two games left, following a 3–1 home victory against Bristol Rovers. The worrying thing about that game was that, despite its importance, we were only watched by 3,220, which was the lowest attendance for any of our games since our promotion.

One of the contributory factors to the poor support was the fact that, unlike other seasons, we seemed incapable of winning at home, registering only five league wins at the Racecourse, the lowest number in the history of the club.

Of course, because of the close proximity of Manchester United and City, Liverpool and Everton, attracting big gates has always been a problem for Wrexham. That season we averaged just over 6,000 per game and when you compare that with some of the clubs we played in the Second Division, you begin to realise what Wrexham were up against. We started the season with a 2–2 draw against Chelsea, in front of 20,000 fans and our final away game of the season was a 0–1 defeat by West Ham in front of 30,515 at Upton Park. While Chelsea and West Ham were the biggest crowds we played in front of, a total of nine clubs in the division had five-figure attendances for our visit, with Derby, Sheffield Wednesday and Newcastle United all attracting gates in excess of 15,000.

When we won promotion into the Second Division we went up with great expectancy and self-belief. We thought that because we had defeated top teams in Cup competitions over the years, we would be able to repeat the process week in, week out in the league. Of course, we soon began to realise it doesn't work like that. These were clubs who were used to higher standards of play for years. Just because we had defeated them once in a Cup match didn't mean that we would be victorious every time we played them.

I suppose it would be very easy to write off Wrexham as a mediocre team, and rubbish what they had achieved. But we must also remember that the team represented the smallest town in the Football League, so all in all they had a history of which they could be proud.

As well as being naïve in our new division, perhaps we concentrated too much on our Cup exploits in England, Wales and Europe and this made our form in the league suffer. Over the years Wrexham have defeated 13 teams from the top division including Spurs, Arsenal, Nottingham Forest, Middlesborough and West Ham. In the 1980–1 season we were to have one slice of Cup glory despite our disappointing form in the league.

In the previous season, as a Second Division side, West Ham United had won the FA Cup by defeating Arsenal in the final at Wembley. They were definitely the best side in our division and proved that by finishing the season as champions. We were drawn against them in the third round, away at Upton Park. In front of 30,000 fans, we fought hard and gave a really disciplined display, especially in defence. We fell behind in the second half to a Ray Stewart penalty and, despite battling hard, we just couldn't find the equaliser until, with three minutes left on the clock, Gareth Davies, not renowned for his goal scoring, smashed one in to bring the Hammers back to the Racecourse.

The replay went into extra time but even after an extra thirty minutes, it was still goalless at the end. This was before the introduction of penalty shoot-outs to settle a stalemate. Normally, the second replay would be on a neutral ground, probably half way between the two teams. At the final whistle the referee talked with the two managers, John Lyall and Arfon Griffiths, and it was agreed that they would toss a coin to see where the second replay should be held. Arfon called correctly, so it meant that for the third match of this tie, we would have home advantage at the Racecourse. The West Ham players were not happy. They were aware of our record in the Cup and, having just had two huge battles against us, I don't think they fancied another trip to north Wales. They were furious that John Lyall had agreed to the tossing of a coin and would have preferred the next match to have been on a neutral ground.

For the second replay, nearly 15,000 fans turned up at the Racecourse. They saw another tense and tight encounter. Early in the match Alan Dwyer hobbled off with an injury. Arfon moved me to the left back position, in place of Alan. The crowd were quite shocked to see me go so far back on the field. Unknown to them, whenever I played five-a-side football, I always played in that position. In those friendly games I enjoyed being there, as there was no pressure on me. When you are a striker, there is a huge expectance from players, management and fans that you will score. It is not so intense when you are a defender, and what is lovely about playing at the back is that you can see everything happen in front of you. When you are up front, all the action is taking place behind you. It's more difficult to read the game and you have to be a lot fitter and faster.

In my new role I ended up marking Alan Devonshire, the England international. He was full of pace and a great player. As he hugged the right wing, he looked over to me and I shouted, "If you come over here, I'll kick you into the stands." Early in the second half he wandered over to the other side of the field. I felt very satisfied and told myself, "Job done." As a player I wasn't a thug, but in those days it was much easier to go in with a tough tackle. Players didn't writhe on the ground in agony, nor did referees go straight for the book. Actually, in that game, the referee, Neil Midgley, was the best I have ever played under.

For the third time in a row, the match was all-square at the end of the ninety minutes, so once again we went into extra time. Just a minute before half-time in the added period, Les Cartwright took a shot at goal. It was deflected into my path by Billy Bonds. Twelve yards from the goal, I stroked the ball into the right hand corner of the net, past the left hand of the goalkeeper, Parkes. As I turned to celebrate the goal, Les Cartwright caught up with me and said, "What the hell are you doing up here? You're supposed to be left back." For the last fifteen minutes we held on to our 1–0 lead and progressed into the fourth round. There we met Wimbledon, a side who had only recently been promoted from the Southern League.

Because our tie against West Ham had taken so long to settle, we played the fourth round match just five days after our third replay with the Hammers. In what was our first ever meeting with the south London club, they gave us a hard fight and when they reduced the deficit to 1–2 with twenty minutes to go, we knew that we were in for a grandstand finish.

In the fifth round match, away to First Division Wolverhampton Wanderers, we took a twenty-ninth minute lead through Steve Fox and held on to it until twenty minutes from the end. Urged on by 8,000 Wrexham fans in the 33,000 crowd, we really should have won the game. Although we didn't play particularly well, neither did Wolves, but in the last twenty minutes we caved in and lost 1–3. Travelling to Molineux before the game, we had all been up for the match and really fancied our chances. I don't think I had all that many bad games for Wrexham, but this was definitely one of my poorest performances and I think that was a view that was shared by the other players of their own performances too. It was certainly a view shared by Arfon. Speaking after the match, he said, "If ever a sixth round place was there to be won, it was today. Wolves were shaky at the back, but we did not expose them enough."

After our Cup exit, it was hoped that we could put together a good run and climb the league. We were particularly keen to start winning at home again, something which we hadn't done since October, when we defeated Bristol City 1–0. Unfortunately, we and the fans had to wait until April, when we trounced highly-placed Sheffield Wednesday 4–0. After that great win, we were hopeful that we could put a good run together to the end of the season. Unfortunately, it was not to be, and in our last five games we won only once, although it was an important 3–1 win at home against Bristol Rovers, which meant that we were safe for another season as a Second Division side.

Apart from the Cup victory over West Ham United, there was one other highlight to the season, which came in September when we beat Derby County at the Baseball Ground. This game will always be remembered for the wonder strike from Ian Edwards. Twenty yards from the goal, he received a pass from Les Cartwright and, despite it being at an acute angle, he smashed the ball with tremendous precision, past the goalkeeper. The *Match of the Day* cameras were at the ground and, not only did it win the Goal of the Month competition, but it was also placed highly for Goal of the Season. I suppose the fact that I finished as top scorer with fifteen goals was a personal highlight.

Apart from the disappointment of our league performances, the greatest shock came a week after we had played our final game of the season at home to

Watford. At every football club there are always rumours that do the rounds, and there had certainly been some rumblings, but it still came as a terrible shock when Arfon Griffiths announced that he was resigning as manager.

With the gates plummeting throughout the season, the financial situation at the club worsened as the season progressed. The chairman, Fred Tomlinson, told Arfon that he would have to shed two of his four backroom staff – Mel Sutton, George Showell, Mickey Evans and Ken Roberts. In a statement, Arfon said, "I have finished because I was not prepared to take the cuts. The directors wanted to reduce my staff and I thought it would be detrimental to the future success of the club. The Board had valid points about the cuts, but so did I. I won't be at the Racecourse again, unless I'm working for someone else."

The statement from the club's Board read: "The Board have made their decision with reluctance. Arfon has been a wonderful servant of the club. His playing record was brilliant and, as a manager, he took the club to the Second Division and has kept it there, despite the most appalling state of injuries among his players. His honesty and integrity are exemplary and everyone at the club will be hoping that he will soon find happiness and success elsewhere."

Along with many others associated with the club, I was gutted when he left. Arfon had brought me to the club and I had grown very close to him – it's a friendship that has continued to the present day. He had been a great player for Wrexham and Wales and also a good manager. There was always a great camaraderie between him and the team. Because of his management style there were never any disruptive players in the dressing room. Since taking over the managerial reins in 1977, he had made it feel as if everyone had a part in the exciting story together. There was no one who felt too big for the club.

The Board had said that they hoped Arfon would find happiness at another club, but I don't think he ever did. He left the Racecourse to manage Crewe Alexandra, but I got the feeling that his heart and soul were never in it. He stayed there a couple of years and then left. He was very much Mr Wrexham, having been at the club all his playing career, except for a very brief stint at First Division Arsenal. During his time at Cresty Road, I think he came to realise that he didn't want to be involved with any other club.

For the 1981–2 season, the Board appointed Mel Sutton as manager. We made a terrible start and, after our first five games, had failed to win with only one point gained from a goalless draw away to Leyton Orient. We stayed in the relegation zone for most of the season, but then, following on from a 1–0 home victory over Chelsea, we were undefeated in the next seven games. During that run we beat top teams such as Newcastle United and Bolton Wanderers. Arthur Cox, the manager of Derby County who drew 1–1 with us at the Racecourse, was amazed that we were in such a plight in the league and said after the game that there was one team every year, in every division, which did not deserve to be in the relegation fight. As far as he was concerned, we were that team in the Second Division. That good run meant that by mid April, we were in fifteenth position and we were beginning to think that we would be safe. But then, a dismal run of only one win in our last eight matches meant that we slipped into the Third Division. It was amazing that, on 20 April 1982, I should make my 500th Football League appearance against Leicester City, the club where it had all started for me, all those years before. The game, which was at the Racecourse, ended goalless and I would have marked my anniversary with a goal if it hadn't been for a fantastic save by the Foxes keeper, Mark Wallington.

The highlight of such a depressing season had to be our FA Cup third round match at the County Ground against Brian Clough's Nottingham Forest. They had won the previous season's European Cup, so the tie pitted a club at the bottom of the Second Division against the top team in Europe. Due to illness Cloughie was not at the game, so his assistant Peter Taylor was in charge of the team. We were 0–1 down after just two minutes. Mark Proctor took a free kick from about twenty-five yards and the ball struck me on its way past Eddie Niedzwiecki in goal. Lots of people in the ground must have thought that this would be the start of Forest running riot. At half-time we were still only trailing by the one goal, but in the second half we played them off the park. Steve Fox had a brilliant game and made goals for Steve Dowman and myself. Mick Vinter scored in between and we ran out 3–1 winners. I was particularly pleased with my goal because I volleyed it past Peter Shilton. It wasn't just because I had played with him at Leicester, but it was also something to do with the fact that he was an international goalie who happened to be the number one keeper in England. It was an incredible result, but unfortunately, didn't save us from the drop.

In footballing terms, it's a long way from Forest's ground to Marine, who then played in the North West Counties League. Strangely, both places were to make a big impact on my season. Colin Edwards was now playing for Marine, having once been on our books at the Racecourse. He asked Wrexham to play at his testimonial match and, during the game, I was involved in an accidental clash of heads. It left me very dazed and I think that George Showell, our physio, and I knew straight away that it was fairly serious.

On the team bus I felt terrible and told George, "My teeth and jaw are screaming at me." George said, "I can't give you anything, you might be sick." In the end he did, and I was. When I got home I just sat in a chair for hours feeling sorry for myself and in agony. The next morning, the X-ray confirmed that I had fractured my cheek bone. It meant that I was unable to play and missed a huge chunk of the season. I was gutted that I got such a serious injury in a match that wasn't important in terms of our league season. I missed thirteen league games and scored just eleven goals. My injury and the club's relegation into the Third Division made the season one to forget. We all hoped that we could turn things around and bounce straight back into the Second Division during the next season.

8

Goodbye pitch, Hello dugout

AT THE END of our relegation season the club sacked Mel Sutton. I talked to Fred Tomlinson, the chairman and asked whether he thought there was any point in me applying for the manager's job. Fred felt I should leave it a couple of years before thinking of management, and the club appointed Bobby Roberts for the start of the 1982–3 season.

I had been at Filbert Street as an apprentice when Bobby was in the Leicester City squad. Despite that link, we didn't seem to hit it off when he came to the Racecourse. I still don't know why that was and often wonder if he discovered that I had been after his job before he arrived. In the previous season, I'd been appointed club captain and I was ready to lead the team out at Farrar Road for a friendly against Bangor City, when Bobby turned to Joey Jones and told him that he was the captain.

Joey was visibly upset and turned to me and said, "Do you know anything about this?" and I assured him that I didn't. The whole incident left me angry and disappointed. Surely Bobby would have had the courtesy to have a word with me privately before the game, and not humiliate me in front of all the other players. I felt the same way at our first league game away to Cardiff City. I got caught in a tackle and was cut just above the ankle. I got the impression that Bobby wanted me to come off, but I persuaded him to leave me on the pitch and I was rewarded by getting the winner eighteen minutes from time, although it was a very scrappy goal.

On another occasion a television crew came to the training ground to interview me. Bobby had organised a training match between the first team and the Reserves. By the time I returned from talking to the interviewer, I was in the Reserves!

Fred Tomlinson spoke with me and told me that because of the salary I was on, the club could no longer afford to keep me. He also informed me that Hereford United wanted to sign me. It never ceases to amaze me how coincidences have played such a big part in my football career. Back in the 1960s I was to make my Football League debut as an Exeter City player in a match at the Racecourse. Now, on 9 October 1982, I found myself making my last appearance in the league as a Wrexham player against Exeter City in a 1–2 defeat. As already mentioned, it was also incredible that I made my 500th Football League appearance against my old club, Leicester City.

After being told that Hereford wanted to sign me, I rang their chairman, Peter Hill. He told me that the club wanted me to be joint manager with Tommy Hughes. For two days I thought long and hard about the offer and then telephoned to say I couldn't see how joint management could work, but was happy to sign as a player.

So, a week after bowing out as a Wrexham player, I played for the Bulls at Edgar Street. They had made a terrible start to their Fourth Division season and were bottom of the league having failed to win in their first nine games. Although I didn't mark my return with a goal, I did hit the bar and the post and I like to think my presence inspired the boys to their first win, a 1–0 victory over Crewe Alexandra.

Going back to Hereford didn't turn out to be the fairy tale return I and everyone else had hoped for. With Dana and the boys settled in Wrexham, I had managed to remain living in the town. Wrexham allowed me to train with them and then, at the weekend, I would travel to Hereford. I began to feel it was unfair on the Herefordshire side and one day, after a long run in Erddig Park, I sat in the bath at home and decided to retire. I talked to Tommy Hughes and explained the situation. So, on 3 January 1983, I played my last league game, which was a 2–1 home victory against Aldershot.

In the 1980s, the PFA ran a benevolent fund which was used to make payments to players when they retired. Because I had been a professional for nineteen years, I was given a cheque for the grand sum of £1,500. A week after receiving the payment, Chester City contacted me to ask whether I would consider playing for them. It transpired that because I had been given this payment, I was banned from playing professionally ever again. You weren't even allowed to hand it back and then play. I suppose you could say that as far as Wrexham Football

Club fans are concerned, that legislation saved my bacon and prevented me from signing for the enemy.

Once retired from the game, I concentrated on my business which makes fireplaces from natural stone and slate. In addition, I started doing some expert analysis for Radio Wales at football matches. I couldn't completely get rid of the playing bug and I signed for Chirk AAA, an amateur side who played in the Welsh National League, Wrexham area. They were a great bunch of lads at the club and were managed by John Green. I found it fun to go back to grass roots football. In many ways it was like returning to where it had all started for me, all those years earlier, playing for Holwell Works in the Leicestershire League. John Green, the Chirk manager, couldn't believe it when I turned up at the ground for my first match, an hour before kick-off. I did this for every game, as I found it impossible to get rid of my professional attitude towards football. The approach obviously paid off in some way, as Chirk won the First Division Championship. The regulars at my local pub, the Fairfield Tavern, asked me to play for their Sunday League team managed by Dennis Williams. So, in my so-called retirement from the game, I ended up playing on Saturday and Sunday.

Wrexham Football Club had a bad season in 1984–5. For most of the year they were bottom of the Fourth Division. In March, after a 1–3 defeat to Tranmere Rovers at Prenton Park, manager Bobby Roberts was dismissed. George Showell took over as caretaker manager and, after eleven games in control, Wrexham had won six and drawn two of their games, lifting them from one place off the bottom to seventeenth. One Friday evening, I was reading the local paper when I noticed that the club were interviewing for the vacant manager's post, the following Monday.

I sat with the paper for a long time and wondered what I should do. As a player, I had always wanted to end my career with Wrexham and now there was a chance to manage them. Of course, there were lots of things to be considered. A few years earlier I had been rebuffed by Fred Tomlinson, who had told me I was too young and didn't have enough experience. I didn't want to be dismissed again. Besides, I had started doing more and more broadcasting for Radio Wales and there was also my business to consider.

I suppose I was like a typical striker coming in at the far post, so I decided to ring Neville Dickens, a director at the club. Still smarting from the Fred Tomlinson treatment, I told him I only wanted to apply if there was a chance of an interview. He told me that the club's Board would love to see me and invited me for an interview on the Monday evening.

As the Board quizzed me, there were several references to the problems I would inherit if I were successful. One Board member said to me, "You come here every week. You know the problems. How many would you get rid of if you were the manager?" I played for time and told them that I would make one or two changes.

Despite all the doubts I had raised when reading the newspaper a few nights earlier, I was really chuffed when I was offered the job. It was like a dream come true. Having been out of the professional game for a couple of seasons, it felt like I was being given the chance to start all over again.

My first game in charge was to be away at Bury on

the Saturday. I had one slight problem which I felt I had to clear with the Board. The Sunday League team, for whom I played, had reached the final of the Shelley Cup which was scheduled for the day after the Bury match at the Racecourse. One or two of the Board members felt that it wouldn't be a good idea for the newly unveiled manager to turn out the next day for the Fairfield Tavern. At first they refused me permission, but then, after a little persuasion, they changed their minds.

When we went to Gigg Lane for my first game as manager, Bury had already been promoted to the Third Division. A great 3–2 victory, with goals from Ian Edwards, Dave Gregory and Shaun Cunnington was followed by a 1–0 home success over Aldershot and a goalless draw away to Blackpool, another team which had been promoted. The victory away at Bury meant that we secured our status as a Fourth Division club. After my first three games at the helm, it also meant that the club had been undefeated in their last eight games. Despite those encouraging statistics, there were also lots of reasons to be concerned.

It was difficult to believe that less than ten years earlier, Wrexham had been playing at the Racecourse in front of crowds of over 15,000, both in League and Cup matches. For my home debut as the new manager, less than 2,000 turned out for the match against Aldershot in 1989. I was also concerned about the style of play. As a player at Hereford and Wrexham, I had enjoyed seven seasons of fast, open football with plenty of goals. My philosophy had always been that if you were within a sniff of goal, you should shoot and have a go. Watching the boys play, I felt that we tip-tapped the ball too much in front of goal. The strikers were not selfish enough;

no one was prepared to take a chance. As far as I was concerned, the fun of football was to score goals. These boys were missing out, and I told Jim Steel I expected twenty goals from him in the forthcoming season. I also wanted to know why, when he had the ball in the goal area, he would often cross it instead of trying to hit the target.

Although the Board had warned me that I would have to get rid of players, it was still very difficult for me when it came to talking to ground staff boys. These were young lads who had set their hearts on careers as footballers and no doubt dreamt of the big time. It was now my job to talk to five of them in turn, and tell them that they had no future at the club; we just didn't have the money to keep them on. I challenged each one and told them that I hoped that one day they would come back and haunt me by turning out as top professionals. Despite trying to encourage them, each one of them left my office in tears. I felt terrible as I watched them go.

The previous season Mike Hooper had done a good job between the posts for Wrexham. He had been on loan from Bristol City and before the season started I tried to buy him. Terry Cooper was manager of the West Country side and he valued Mike at £15,000. I thought he must be having me on, as Mike was their fourth choice keeper, so I offered £2,000. But Terry wasn't joking, and so the matter went before a football tribunal. The panel was chaired by George Curtis of Coventry City and Terry Cooper went in first to make his case, and then I followed him.

When George Curtis called us back in to tell us the tribunal's findings, he informed us that the fee was set at £4,000. I thought that was an absolute steal, as Mike was a great goalkeeper. Although it was a good price, there was still the little problem of how we would raise the money. As a club we were totally skint and that thought was obviously going through the minds of Board members Joe Scott and Gordon Mytton, who had accompanied me to the hearing. As George Curtis stated the price, the two Board members shouted out, "Fucking hell, how are we going to afford that?"

Once everyone (other than the members of the tribunal) had left the room, I was asked to go back in and talk to them. They told me that I had given a good presentation but they had not been so impressed with Gordon and Joe. They asked me to tell them that if they ever spoke like that at a future tribunal, they would be fined.

By the end of August in the 1985–6 season, we had won three of our first four games, drawn the other and were third in the league. The team's performances earned me the Manager of the Month award. Mike Hooper played a total of fourteen consecutive games for us but, during that period, some of our performances were erratic. At the end of September, I was fuming after a totally unprofessional display against Leyton Orient at home, a match we lost 1–3. Our inconsistency was shown when we followed that performance with a good 2–1 away win at Northampton, after which we went to Port Vale where we were thrashed 0–4. Just ten days after that disaster, we beat Cambridge United 6–2 at home. Two days after that Tuesday night victory, I was called to a meeting of the club's Board. I was told that Liverpool had put in a bid for Mike Hooper and that they were willing to pay £50,000. Because of our dreadful financial situation, the

Board were determined to sell him, but they also told me that the First Division outfit wanted Mike the next day. That left me with a terrible dilemma. I had little or no cover for the goalkeeper. Mark Morris was on our books, but he was a youngster who was totally inexperienced at the professional level. In two days we had a game at the Recreation Ground against Aldershot. I asked the Board to tell Liverpool that they would have to wait until the following Monday, but some of the members were afraid that the club would withdraw the offer. In the end, I won the argument and we managed to keep Liverpool's offer a secret, so that Mike Hooper played in the Aldershot match. We conceded two goals in the first half, lost Jim Steel in the twentieth minute and completely caved in during the last quarter of the game, so we were thrashed 0–6.

As the players traipsed off the pitch, I asked Mike to join me in the dugout. He sat next to me, looking incredibly sad. He then started reliving the nightmare of the match, going through the goals one by one. "I'm sorry gaffer," he said, "I really couldn't stop any of them." I had to put him out of his misery and tell him the news that as a club we had kept under wraps for two days. There are not many goalies who can concede six goals in a Fourth Division match and then sign for one of the top teams in Europe on the same day.

Mike Hooper's departure left me without a goalkeeper and our next match was the derby game away to Chester City the following Saturday. That week I seemed to spend most of my time on the phone, ringing various clubs to see if they had a goalie available. As one manager after another told me that they couldn't help me, I said to myself, welcome to management at the lowest level. Perhaps the most colourful refusal came from Ron Atkinson, then manager of Sheffield Wednesday. It turned out that the goalkeeper I was hoping to sign was injured.

"What do you want him for?" Big Ron asked.

"To save shots," I replied.

"At this club all the keepers can save shots, but none of them can catch the fucking ball," was his curt reply.

As time started to run out, I signed an amateur stopper from the Welsh National League, Wrexham area, the same division as I had played in for Chirk AAA. Mike Keen joined us from Lex XI and just when it seemed I would have to pitch an inexperienced player between the posts for the derby game, I managed to get John Vaughan on loan from West Ham United. After making his debut in the 1–1 draw at Chester, John Vaughan was to play only three more games for the club, as West Ham did not want him to get Cup tied.

The fact that I had to use five different keepers in the league that season, shows what a problem I had with the number one position. After Vaughan returned to the First Division, we used Mike Keen and Mark Morris, until Don Ferguson joined us on an indefinite trial. He had played in the Canadian Olympic football team in 1984, and came to the Racecourse after he had been turned down by Luton Town. By making twenty appearances, he brought some stability to the defence and the club.

That first season in charge was a constant battle against injuries to a small squad, and the continuing financial crisis, which was never helped by the low number of spectators that came through the turnstiles. The game which highlighted the difficulties we faced as a club was the FA Cup second round replay against Notts County. We drew 2–2 away, but for the return encounter at the Racecourse I knew we would struggle, as I was missing five of my twelve professionals. Before the game I chatted with George Showell as we realised that one of us would have to put our name down on the teamsheet as a substitute. In the end, I drew the short straw and my name went down. We were 0–2 down with twenty minutes to play when John Muldoon was carried off, injured. I realised that I would have to go on and thought it was worth giving it a try. As a thirty-seven year old trotting on to the pitch, I soon realised that my head was up for the challenge, but my body wasn't so certain. It didn't take me very long to realise that I shouldn't be out there. When you don't train regularly, then you have no chance of making an impression. It took me even less time to realise that I would have to run off the pitch to the dugout again as I had left my false teeth in. It was essential to take them out before starting to play.

I suppose you could say that that first season as a manager was a huge adventure, often an adventure into the unknown. As a side we were in desperate need of a left winger. I often used to watch Liverpool Reserves and, on one occasion, I phoned Kenny Dalglish and told him I was interested in the young boy I had seen streaming down the left flank. His name was Steve McManaman. Unfortunately, Kenny saw great potential in the player too, and was not keen for us to sign him, but sent us Brian Mooney instead.

As my first year in charge drew to a close, although there had been lots of ups and downs and pressures, I was still thrilled to be the manager of a club that meant so much to me. Even after a defeat and a long journey home in the dark, as the bus pulled off the bypass and I saw the floodlights, I would be proud of the great stadium we had, especially when you compared it to some of the other grounds in our division.

The one highlight of that first season was the fact that we won the Welsh Cup. In the final we met Kidderminster Harriers, who were then a non-league side. Although we were the Football League side, they had far more money than us. Their two strikers, Kim Casey and Paul Davies, who scored goals for fun, were earning far more than anyone at the Racecourse. The first leg at home had ended as a draw and Kidderminster must have fancied their chances of lifting the trophy on their own ground, but we beat them 2–1.

During that first full season in charge, I used five goalkeepers in league games. However, for the Welsh Cup matches, I had an ace up my sleeve as I called up my best mate Dai Davies who had retired from football. I ended up drafting him in because Mike Keen was Cup tied. I am convinced that it helped us to win the Welsh Cup. Dai was superb at talking to defenders, organising those in front of him and being in charge of the goal area.

I realised how important winning the Welsh Cup was for the club that night. Qualifying once again for the European Cup Winners' Cup was essential. Financially, we were on our knees and a tie against a top team would help us enormously. In the first round we were drawn against Zureq, the Cup winners from Malta. After a comfortable 4–0 aggregate victory, we were amazed when the draw for the second round was announced. Our opponents were to be the crack Spanish side, Real

Zaragoza, who had beaten the mighty Barcelona in the Spanish Cup final.

Just before we left for Spain, we had played Southend United at the Racecourse, in front of 900 people, which was the lowest attendance in the history of the club. It was incredible to think that we would be going from that to a crowd of 25,000 in Spain. After arriving in the country by aeroplane we were then taken by coach to the hotel. The journey seemed to last forever and we all felt jaded when we arrived. On the night of the match, I was giving a team talk at 7.15 p.m. when the door opened. The directors of the club, who all appeared a little worse for wear, due to Spanish wine rather than the long journey, came in to wish the players well. One of them said, "Please don't lose 0–6 or else we'll never get a crowd at the Racecourse." The boys battled fantastically and defended brilliantly against a side which included Sosa, who had cost them £2 million. He exuded class but we managed to return to Wales with a goalless draw. Only Jim Steel hitting the crossbar stopped us from having an amazing win.

When we returned to Wrexham, I began to think about the game out in Spain. Zaragoza were obviously a stylish and talented side. They played the ball wide and were able to pull defences out of position and then exploit the space they created. I amazed our groundsman, Johnny Edwards, by telling him that I wanted the pitch to be marked again. I felt that if we set the markings to the minimum width, then that could frustrate our Spanish visitors. So that's what we did. We narrowed the pitch by ten yards.

The anxious Board members who had stormed into

the dressing room before the game in Spain, needn't have worried. Over 14,000 fans poured into the Racecourse for the second leg. While it was great to see such a crowd and to hear them in full voice cheering on the boys, I couldn't help but wonder where had they been when we were playing the likes of Southend and Aldershot. The players again gave their all and, in a thrilling game, we came from behind on two occasions, to earn an incredible 2–2 draw against the respected continental side. Although we went out of the European Cup Winners' Cup because of the away goal rule, it was another fantastic Cup night to remember at the Racecourse.

Away from the excitement of those two matches, life in the Fourth Division continued to be a struggle. I seemed to spend the whole season wheeling and dealing, trying to bring in quality players with no money to pay for them. I used a total of twenty-two players for the forty-six league games and seven of my players were semi-professional. We finished in ninth place, but were let down by our home form. We drew thirteen of our twenty-three home games and if we could have converted those draws into victories, then we would have walked the division and been promoted into the Third Division.

The most memorable league game of that season was at Spotland against Rochdale. It was a game I will never forget – but for all the wrong reasons. It turned out to be a fairly farcical encounter with a referee who clearly didn't know what he was doing. It was his first game as a professional referee and I'm afraid it showed.

The game ended with the home side beating us 3–2. One of Rochdale's goals went through a tear in the back of the net and, as the home players celebrated, the official ran to the goal line, peered into the net and said, "Yes there is definitely a hole in the net."

With the score level at 2–2, our keeper, John Vaughan, came out and caught the ball. Their striker challenged John and knocked the ball out of his hands and kicked the ball into the back of our net for the winning goal. Incredibly, the referee had his back to the goal and didn't see the incident. The linesman flagged to show that the Rochdale player had committed a foul, and the goal should be disallowed. The referee, seeing the flag, went over to talk to his linesman and the next thing was that he put his flag down and the 'goal' was allowed to stand.

I could see what had happened, and I was so furious I began to argue with the linesman. The referee could see that I was quarreling and he came over to the touchline and told me to sit down in the dugout. I did, but I was still fuming about the decision.

It was a crisp November Saturday afternoon. I had to take out my anger on someone or something. Nearby was a plastic bucket which George Showell, the physio, had been using. I leapt up and kicked it sky high. I have never seen anything quite like what happened next. The bucket exploded in midair. At the split second it disintegrated, a policeman appeared to investigate the disturbance I was creating. The water from the bucket covered him from head to foot! I have never been threatened with so many dreadful things by a man of the law. I'm just relieved that he was wearing a fairly thick winter coat.

The next season, when we returned for the repeat

fixture, I told George Showell that I felt I should buy the Rochdale club a present to show that I was sorry about what had happened the previous year. I got them a new galvanised bucket and inscribed it with the words 'Please do not kick me, as it happened once before. Merry Xmas!'

The difficulties I had fought against in all my years in charge at Wrexham surfaced again in the next season, 1987–8. The club was still heavily in debt and, if the previous season had been dominated by our European Cup adventures, this one was the year in which I was constantly forced to sell good players. Paul Constive and goalkeeper Chris Pearce had been two very dependable performers in the previous season. They travelled in every day for training from Burnley where they both lived. They asked for a rise in their wages to help pay for their travel expenses. When I put their case to Gordon Mytton of the Board, he told me that there was no money available. The best I could offer them was a £5 a week rise in their income. They refused the offer and we lost them as they both signed for Burnley.

The previous year I had fought off various offers for Barry Horne, an outstanding midfielder who had been capped by Wales. Because of the financial difficulties, I finally had to let him go and he was signed by First Division Portsmouth.

Among all the departures there was one signing which pleased me. The club secretary, Tony Rance, told me to have a look at player called Kevin Russell. I went to see him play for Portsmouth Reserves and was impressed. He was a twenty-year-old footballer who had played for England Youth. Playing on the right wing he had tremendous pace and was able to strike the ball with both feet. We signed him for £10,000 and played him at centre forward instead of on the wing. In his first season, he scored twenty-one goals and as a manager you know that the club can go somewhere with that kind of performance.

Our dreadful financial situation didn't just mean that we had to sell players, such as Chris Pearce and Paul Constive, who had been at the club for a while; it also meant that it was hard to hold on to footballers who had joined us on loan. In his earlier career Jimmy Harvey had played for Arsenal and had been an Irish international. He was a commanding player in the middle of the field and, because of his great skills, he could open doors for the forwards and split defences with superb passes. Jimmy joined us from Bristol City and when he made his debut against Cardiff, which we won 3–0, we were just three places off the bottom of the Fourth Division. After six games playing for us, we had climbed to thirteenth in the table. I wanted to sign him, but of course we didn't have the money. He signed for Tranmere Rovers and later in the season he was joined by Jim Steel, whom the Birkenhead club bought for £50,000. Sean Cunnington, who had played 199 times for Wrexham, was signed by Bobby Roberts and joined Grimsby Town for another £50,000.

In the New Year, I was told that Dave McKay at Doncaster was prepared to release Brian Flynn to us. Although he was nearing the end of his playing career, he still had a lot to offer and was a class player. After a dismal start to the season, when we were hammered 6–1 at Plainmoor by Torquay United and had long stretches near the foot of the table, we were able to turn things around and finished eleventh. An unbeaten run through March and April, during which time we won six consecutive matches, helped us climb the table.

There is little doubt that the highlights of our league season were the two victories over Wolverhampton Wanderers. The Wolves had slipped down through the divisions and found themselves in football's bottom tier for the first time in their history. At Molineux the boys gave a great performance and we came away with a 2–0 victory. I remember coming out of the ground wondering, "How on earth did we win that one?"

Wolves were easily the best team in the division and proved it later on by winning the Championship. They had some great players and really outplayed us for the ninety minutes. But somehow, we dug in and held on and Mike Williams had a fabulous game in defence. I always think that Mike was one of the most underrated players at the Racecourse. He was a first-class defender and gave his all in every game. He didn't get the credit he deserved and I was sad when he had to retire from the game because of knee problems. I am convinced that, had he not suffered such serious injuries, he would have played at the highest level.

At Molineux we beat Wolves despite the fact that they were undefeated in eleven games. When they came to the Racecourse, they had already been promoted and were chasing the Championship. Our crowd of nearly 7,000 was the highest that the Racecourse had seen since our Second Division days. Steve Bull, who had scored thirty goals, had a quiet afternoon and we defeated them 4–2 in a cracking game.

Despite the fact that we had an encouraging end

to the season, with only two defeats in our last eleven games, our crowds were the fourth worst in the entire Football League. Only Halifax Town, Rochdale and Newport County (who were demoted from the Football League) were watched by fewer people. Many of the early games in the season attracted gates of well under 2,000 and only bumper crowds against big teams such as Wolves (6,898) and Bolton Wanderers (5,997) brought the average to as high as it was.

The lack of support and the continuing financial battles at the club, forced general manager, Tony Rance, to state at the beginning of the 1988-9 season: "The income that we are getting from attendances is not equating to players' wages and the costs of running the club. We really must start making ends meet."

We made a goodish start to the new season with an away victory at St James' Park against Exeter City (2–0) and then a 3–0 home victory over Lincoln City. It was strange to start the new campaign with wins over two of my old clubs. But then, after the bright start, our form slumped. We went seven games without a win but managed to stop the rout with a 3–1 win away to Hartlepool United. This was the start of an unbeaten run of twelve games, and we rose from the bottom half of the table into the play-off positions.

Our run of good form came to an end though when Lincoln City beat us 4–3 at Sincil Bank in mid January. From the end of March we went on another bad run with only one victory in eight games. With only three games left to the end of the season, we were in seventh position, the final play-off place, and were in serious danger of missing out on the play-offs and our chance of promotion to the Third Division. We followed a 2–1 win away to Carlisle United with two home victories against Torquay United (1–0) and Rochdale (2–1). During that final game, everyone was listening to their pocket radios to make sure that Cambridge United didn't pip us to the final play-off spot. I told the press after the game, "The second half was a long forty-five minutes. I was trying to keep calm but it was very difficult. We did not play as well as we can, but in the end we got the result. If that's only qualifying, God knows what the play-offs will be like."

We easily disposed of Scunthorpe United in the play-off semi-final, winning 3–1 at home and 2–0 away. The first leg of the final was at home to Leyton Orient, which ended in a goalless draw. Over 13,000 crammed into Brisbane Lane, 3,000 of whom had made the long trip down from north Wales to cheer us on. We thought we were going to go into the dressing room all-square, but Lee Harvey scored for the Os one minute before the half-time whistle. Four minutes into the second half, John Bowden equalised with a header from Steve Buxton's cross. For the next thirty minutes I, along with the players and all the fans, really thought we were heading for the Third Division. Whereas the away goal rule had cost us dearly in our games against Real Zaragoza in the Cup Winners' Cup, it now looked as if it would see us through. But then, with only nine minutes left on the clock, the home striker Mark Cooper scored to take Orient up instead of us.

The new season 1989–90 started with the now familiar pattern of star players being sold. Kevin Russell who, in his two seasons with me at the club, had scored a total of forty-five league goals, was sold to Leicester City for

£175,000. Mike Salmon, the goalkeeper, who had been outstanding for us, joined Charlton Athletic for £50,000. I replaced the two with the experienced keeper, Vince O'Keefe, who we signed from Blackburn Rovers and striker, Gary Worthington, from Darlington.

After all the excitement of reaching the play-off final in the previous season, we made a terrible start to the new campaign and won only three games in our first thirteen encounters. Our thirteenth game was a 1–1 draw at home to Torquay United. This was to be my last game as manger of the club, as I announced my resignation.

Many people thought I had left Wrexham because of the bad start we'd made. That was not the reason. After endless struggles to keep the club afloat, I felt worn out. I had had enough. It felt as though the club was not going anywhere and nobody seemed to care.

As far as I was concerned I'd made my decision in the week before the Torquay game and the official announcement. The final straw was our away match the previous week, against Maidstone United. Because of the lack of funds at the club, most of our away travel was made on the day of the match. After looking at the fixture list at the beginning of the season, it was agreed that this game would be the exception. Maidstone was so far away from north Wales that David Rhodes, the secretary, agreed that the club would book us an overnight stay at a hotel. On the Tuesday before the game David Rhodes came to see me and informed me that all the hotels in the area were full. He said that we would have to travel by coach on the day. The next day he broke the news to me that he had been unable to get a coach too.

After discussion, it was agreed that the players would

travel in their own cars to Crewe station and we would then catch the train to London Euston. I pointed out to David Rhodes that, if the players were making this long journey by car and train, it was vital that they should have a good meal before the game. David Rhodes agreed, and he went off to book the pre-match meal. The next day, Thursday, he came to tell me that he had been unable to get a reservation for a meal, and we would just have to go and play.

On the day of the match we piled players and kit into cars. We pulled out of the Racecourse car park at 8 a.m. and headed for Crewe railway station. Once we arrived at Euston, we caught the Underground and then waited for the commuter train to Maidstone. I still have memories of watching my players sitting on benches in the station, eating Mars bars and crisps. That was some pre-match meal. We had to wait an hour for our connecting train. Once we came out of the station in Maidstone, we were greeted by a full-scale storm. The wind was blowing strongly and the rain was lashing down. We decided against walking, and caught taxis to take us to the ground. There were about ten minutes to spare when we turned up at the ground and, considering our preparation, we played fairly well and it was a credit to the players that we only lost 0–2.

After the game we set out on the next leg of our journey from hell. I reckon it took us a total of ten hours by road and rail. I felt really sorry for the players and, on the Sunday, I spent a long time thinking about what we all had to go through. The longer I thought, the more I came to the conclusion that this was no way to treat players or run a professional football club. In many ways, it was no way to run an amateur club.

By the time I got to the club on the Monday, I had decided that I would resign. Gordon Mytton was away, but Pryce Griffiths, another Board member came into the office. Once I had told him about the events of the previous Saturday, I said, "I'm finishing, this is no way to treat professional footballers."

Pryce Griffiths was keen that I should stay as manager of the club. Afraid that I was making a decision because of my anger at the Maidstone incident, he encouraged me to go away and have a long hard think and then let him know my decision in a couple of days. I appreciated his concern but my view didn't change and I decided to leave. I suggested that the Board should consider appointing Brian Flynn or Joey Jones as my successor. I then arranged to speak with the players, and it was finally agreed with the Board that the home game against Torquay United, the following Saturday, would be my last in charge.

I have never been a football mercenary. I could never go to a club, take the wages and carry on regardless of whatever was happening on the field. I have always been driven by the desire to be successful at everything I do. As I looked back on my four seasons of management, I began to realise that you can have all the desire and energy in the world, but if the club hasn't got money, then your team will always finish lower down in the table.

Not long after my decision became official, the old doubts started to surface. You're a fool, I thought to myself, you've walked out on a club that you really loved. I also reminded myself that the club had offered me a new three-year contract which they were waiting for me to sign. As I wondered whether or not I had made a mistake, it was obvious that Dana was unhappy. She was aware of what I had given up and was also concerned about the financial implications of the decision I had just made.

There seemed very little chance of another club inviting me to be their manager. While players tend to move from club to club, there is not the same amount of movement and new opportunities for managers in the lower leagues. Boards tend to offer management to players coming to the end of their playing careers, just as Wrexham did with Brian Flynn once I had left. Despite my lingering doubts, I decided to stand by my decision. I knew it would force me to do something else with my life.

When Dana, Richard and I moved to Wrexham we had spent the previous eleven years moving from place to place. It had felt as though it was the right time to put down proper roots. Our move to Wrexham had coincided with the most successful time in the history of the club. We quickly became accepted by people in Wrexham and made lots of friends. As a small boy Richard had been moved around too many times, and I decided that I had had enough of my life as a nomad. The longer I lived there, the more I realised that Wrexham was my kind of town. Within five minutes you are in breathtaking country and a forty minute drive takes you to the centres of Liverpool or Manchester. Now that I was looking for something else to do, I knew that whatever came along, I didn't want to uproot from Wrexham. I think I am a bit of a country boy at heart, and besides I still had my business in Minera, just a couple of miles outside the town.

9

Farewell Racecourse

JUST AFTER MY resignation, my old friend John Sillett, by now the manager of Coventry City, contacted me and invited me to Highfield Road. He had courted me the previous season when Wrexham made the play-offs. One morning, during a training session with the Wrexham players, I looked across and noticed someone watching us. It was Terry Paine, who was John's assistant. Terry told me that he had been sent to watch me in action and then talk to me, as John was interested in signing me as a coach. I told him that I wasn't interested as, despite all the difficulties, I was enjoying myself at Wrexham and wanted to continue as a manager. At the end of the season, just before our own play-off matches, Coventry City reached the final of the FA Cup at Wembley and played Tottenham Hotspur. John sent me four tickets, for Dana, me and Richard and Jamie. We had a great day and saw Coventry beat Spurs 3–2 in a thrilling final. I will never forget watching John do his unforgettable jig on the Wembley turf, a big man trying to dance and keep his balance and hold the FA Cup at the same time. As I soaked up the atmosphere I couldn't stop myself thinking, if only I'd accepted their offer I could be out there with him – that could have been me holding the Cup...

Now, five months on from Wembley, John was approaching me again. He asked me to go and chat with him and invited me to a First Division match. I was very impressed with the set-up and was tempted to join the staff. But I was determined that I would not move from the Wrexham area. I still wasn't prepared to uproot Dana, Richard and Jamie, or disrupt their lives. John was happy about that arrangement, so I went back into football management, but this time at a top division side, and travelled in from north Wales.

As brilliant as it was to be the first team coach at Coventry, it wasn't the same as being a manager. I couldn't stop thinking about Wrexham Football Club and missed the fact that I was no longer involved with them. After the euphoria of the Cup success, the season for Coventry turned into a battle to avoid relegation into the Second Division. John kept the Sky Blues up and reminded his chairman that it had been in the contract that he would have a pay rise if he kept them in the top division. John's contract was up for renewal and, when he sat to discuss new terms, he was told that there would be no such bonus. I think John and I are similar in that we will always fight for our rights. The chairman's views led to a huge confrontation and in the end John walked away from Highfield Road.

Coventry appointed Terry Butcher, the ex-Ipswich and England centre half, as John's successor. Soon after Terry arrived, I made it clear that I had only joined the club because of my loyalty to John Sillett and Terry Paine. I knew that if I stayed as his coach, then he would expect me to relocate from Wrexham, and I was not prepared to do that. I also realised that he would want to bring in his own back room staff and so, early on in the new season, I left the club.

For the next three years I concentrated on my business and also worked for BBC Wales as a summariser on the Saturday and midweek editions of their sports programmes. Then, I ended up in management again, this time as a result of my son.

Richard, who played up front, had been released by Coventry City, where he was an apprentice. He then signed for Brian Flynn at Wrexham but again, sadly, failed to make the grade and was released by the club. He joined Flint Town United in the Konika League of Wales. Flint were having a poor season and were third from bottom, and Richard couldn't get into the team. He asked me to go and watch him one day and tell him honestly whether I thought he was good enough to be playing for them. So, one afternoon I stood on the far touchline, as far away as possible from the crowd, in the hope that I wouldn't be recognised. At half-time, a person walked over to where I was standing and told me that Alan Baines, the club chairman, would like to invite me to join him for a coffee in the Boardroom. He told me that their manager was retiring and wondered if I would consider becoming their manager. I told him "No thanks" and explained that I didn't want to manage anybody else. Mr Baines was very persistent and he kept pestering me. In the end I gave in, and I made sure that Richard would be in the team, because he was easily good enough. He ended up scoring nineteen goals that season.

Pre-season training in the sand dunes at Borth

1977 and not a grey hair in sight!

Hand ball!

A 1978 portrait

THE GOAL-DEN LEGEND

DIXIE SENT TO COVENTRY

Top job for ex-Racecourse favourite

Dixie McNeil — first division opportunity that escaped him as a player

DIXIE McNeil was today made first team coach at Coventry City. McNeil, 43 next week, quit as Wrexham manager on **October 31.**

He gets a two-year contract at Highfield Road.

The move ends months of whispered speculation reuniting McNeil with Sky Blues' boss, John Sillett.

They were together at Hereford United. Sillett sold McNeil to Wrexham for £60,000 12 years ago.

In an exclusive interview, McNeil said today: "It's a superb club to be involved with. The set up is tremendous, and I'm really looking forward to it."

The timing, however, could have been better.

Coventry crashed out of the FA Cup to third division Northampton — one of McNeil's former clubs — on Saturday.

Last season Sky Blues were ignominiously

EXCLUSIVE INTERVIEW BY DAVID LOVETT

knocked out of the Cup by non-league Sutton United.

But McNeil said "I am joining a first division club which is going in the right direction.

"I am also going to work with a guy whom I have respected for a long, long time. No one, other than John, would have got me away from Wrexham where we have been very happy.

"But I missed out as a player in the first division and the lure has always been there.

"I don't want to miss out this time. The oppor-

tunity is just too good to miss.

"It's going to be a challenge — but that's what life is all about isn't it? I owe it myself to show I can do a job at this level.

"Coventry City may not be the biggest club in the first division — but it equals any club for ambition.

"John is full of it, and I'm just looking forward

to starting work with the players."

Among the top players he will be working with are Cyrille Regis and volatile Scottish international David Speedie.

McNeil said: "Speedie is my type of player — I'm really going to enjoy barking at him"

Coventry manager John Sillett said "I have been looking for a first team coach, which will be his title, for a long time now because you need someone to share the load with you.

Article from *Wrexham Evening Leader*

With Kevin Keegan at my testimonial match at the Racecourse in 1994

Testimonial dinner at Wrexham with my two sons Richard and Jamie and my good friend and former England manager Graham Taylor

David Smallman, me and Gareth Davies at a function for my testimonial match

My mum and dad at Wrexham with their grandson Jamie

Dana and me on our first holiday abroad

My good-looking wife Dana

My great friend Dai Davies, Dana and me at Dai's house in Mold

Dai Davies, Micky Vinter, me and John Roberts with our wives

My best friend Graham Fuller and wife Gillian and *my foot* on the beach in Bournemouth

Dana, little Richard and me outside our new house in Wrexham

Richard, my eldest son with me prior to the game against Arsenal in March 1978

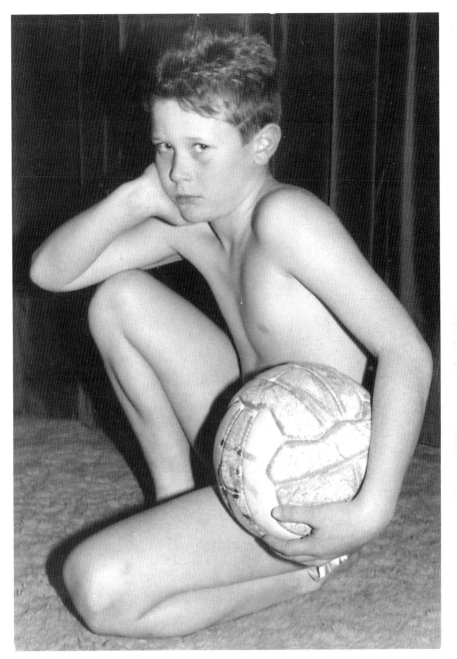

My youngest son Jamie, just after his football kit had been stolen

My son Richard

A family occassion
L–R: Teresa (Jamie's wife), Jamie, Dana, Jackie (Richard's mother-in-law), me, Kerry (Richard's wife) and Richard

My grandsons, Morgan and Jack

Enjoying life as a football pundit with BBC Radio Wales and the lottery manager of Air Ambulance Wales

Flint Town United had some good young players. On the wing they had a fast and exciting player called Alan Evans. Stephan Rush, who was Ian Rush's brother, also played for us. When I took over, the team was third from the bottom of the league, but we managed to turn things around and, by the end of the season, we finished fourth from the top.

After that great start, things fell apart in the 1995–6 season. In that league, Bangor City were the team with loads of money. We knew that when they came looking for some of our good young players, we would have to fight them off. We decided to ask the players to sign contracts. When the Farrar Road side eventually bought Alan Evans, they paid us £3,000 for him, because they thought he was on a contract. The truth of the matter was that neither he, nor any of our team, were on contracts, as we just didn't have the money to offer such deals. The situation we were in led to huge arguments among the committee. Many of them felt that I shouldn't have let Alan Evans go, but I was left with no alternative. One of the committee decided to have a go at me and the team. He complained that we were not playing well away from home.

"How would you know?" I asked, "you've never been to see them play away in the twelve months I've been in charge."

After this exchange there were changes in the committee. Alan Baines left as chairman and I decided to leave also.

*

Four years after leaving Flint Town United, I was talked into taking charge of Caernarfon Town, who were a Welsh League side too. The infighting which had driven me out of Flint was alive and well in Caernarfon also, unfortunately. Against my wishes, they got rid of all the Liverpool-based players and decided to use only local players. Whilst the decision was driven by finances, I felt it would destroy the club.

"If you do that," I told the chairman "we'll go straight down."

"I know we will, but you can bring us straight back up."

The only highlight of that 1999–2000 season was that we reached the quarter-final of the Welsh Premier Cup. It was a competition in which every game was televised. We were drawn away to Swansea City at the Vetch. They were a good team and that season they went on to win the Fourth Division Championship, under John Hollins. Ten days before the tie, the chairman approached me and said: "I'll treble the budget if you sign a brand new team for the Swansea match. I don't want to be humiliated in front of the nation, not on television."

I couldn't believe what I was hearing.

"What are you going to do a week after the game, when all those players go back to their clubs?" I asked him. "Our players who you will have got rid of are not going to come back to Caernarfon and sign again. Why don't you give the extra money to our players?"

Each player was on about £60 for an appearance. With the bonus the club now offered them, they could earn £250 each if they beat Swansea City. After twenty minutes with the game goalless, we scored a wonder goal. I felt we had scored too early and that we would suffer once the Swans got going. Somehow we hung on for seventy minutes and went back to north Wales with a famous 1–0 victory under our belts.

After that famous victory we were drawn in the semi-final to play Cardiff City home and away. We lost 0–3 in both games. I decided to play Jamie and Richard and, for the second leg, I named myself as a substitute. I was tempted to go on for the last five minutes so that father and two sons would play in the same team. But, by the time I got myself ready to take to the pitch, the final whistle had blown!

Despite the fact that the club received £35,000 from the television company for the Swansea game, I got a message from the chairman informing me that the players would not be paid the bonus. All the money would go into the club's coffers. After six weeks of battles, I eventually got the money to pay the players. After that incident, several people came up to me and said, "Get rid of the chairman, I'll take over instead." Yet again I was caught in the middle of internal politics and club infighting. I couldn't stand it, so eventually I walked away and left them to it.

In 2004 I went to help Cefn Newi Druids, another Welsh League side, because my friends Ossie Jones and Graham Jones were involved with the club and they asked me to help them sort things. We did, and that was my last flirtation with non-league management. It left me free to concentrate on my radio broadcasting.

*

The summarising at Wrexham's matches for Radio Wales came completely out of the blue. Ian Gwynne Hughes, one of the presenters on their sports programmes, telephoned me and asked if I would like to summarise at one of the home matches at the Racecourse. I genuinely thought it would just be for the one game and now, twenty-five years on, I am still doing it. If I had known the work was going to last so long, then perhaps I would have learnt Welsh, so that I could also summarise on Radio Cymru. My role has meant that I have ended up travelling to almost every Football League ground in the country and since Wrexham's demise from the league, I have been to several clubs who play in the Blue Square Premier.

One of the most amazing grounds I visited was in the 2010–11 season, when Wrexham were drawn against Eastwood Town in the FA Challenge Trophy. At the Racecourse, the tie had ended all-square, so we all went to Eastwood on the Tuesday night for the replay. The ground was so tiny that they had no facilities for broadcasting. We had to take a portable recording kit, to which we attached a remote transmitter. The only place where we could set this up was on the touchline. Before the match, I stood next to Phil Steele, who was commentating on the game. Away from the security of the commentary box, we were completely surrounded by the home fans. I mentioned that I was surprised that one of Eastwood's players, who had impressed me at the Racecourse, was not playing. As I asked this question live on radio, a man from the crowd shouted, "He's strained his calf muscle." "How do you know that?" I asked. "Because I'm his father," he replied.

Because I am so passionate about all things

connected to Wrexham Football Club, some people have asked me whether I can be neutral when I am summarising at their matches. I don't think there is a problem, as I think it is important to be as objective as possible when you are assessing the match. There are a lot of Wrexham fans who, while they are watching the game live, are also listening to me on the radio. I owe it to them to give as honest a report as possible and I think they would prefer that, rather than me talking a load of passionate gobbledygook.

Despite battling to be neutral, there have been games when I have been the summariser and have been very excited at the end of the game. At the end of April 1993, Brian Flynn's side needed just two points from their last two games to clinch promotion for the first time since I had helped them fifteen years earlier as a player. Around 3,500 Wrexham fans made the long journey to my old club Northampton Town, and they formed a huge part of the crowd of 7,500. Two goals from Gary Bennett gained the points and promotion from Division 3 (the old Fourth Division) into the Second Division. At the end of the game I gave my summary for the radio and then, later, the studio decided to come back to me. The Wrexham fans, who were ecstatic, were making such a din that I couldn't hear a word of the questions coming to me from Cardiff. I just had to guess what they were saying and speak into the mike with my answers to non-existent questions!

The season prior to all those wonderful scenes at Northampton, I was lucky enough to be covering the third round of the FA Cup. It was another case of chalk and cheese taking to the pitch, with little old Wrexham up against the might of Arsenal. When they kicked off,

Wrexham were eighteenth in the Fourth Division, having finished bottom of the league the previous season. Arsenal, on the other hand, were champions of the top division. Leading 1–0 at half-time through an Alan Smith goal, Arsenal played in the second half as if they believed they were already through to the fourth round. I can remember saying on the radio that Arsenal were strolling as if they were in a training session, and that this might give Wrexham a chance. With eight minutes remaining, Mickey Thomas smashed a wonderful free kick into the top right hand corner of the net, past goalkeeper Dave Seaman. That wonder strike from Mickey has been shown again and again on television and I, for one, could carry on watching it forever! Two minutes after his goal, Steve Watkin put Wrexham ahead and, despite Arsenal getting the ball in the back of the Wrexham net, the goal was disallowed and Wrexham progressed to the next round with a famous 2–1 victory. That result has never been forgotten by Wrexham fans, and it still hurts everyone connected with the London club. In 2011, I was at a dinner where Paul Merson, who had laid on the goal for Alan Smith, was the after dinner speaker. When he saw me in the room he said, "As Dixie is here I suppose I will have to talk about that fucking game. Arsenal were useless and Wrexham were useless. The game was a total shambles and that's all I'm going to say about it." As I say, it still hurts them.

The other great moment of my summarising career happened when Wrexham reached the Freight Rover Trophy final at the Millennium Stadium in the 2004–5 season. Off the field it had been a torrid time, as the club fought against the intended asset stripping of Hamilton and Gutterman. The club went into administration and, because of the ten points deducted, they found themselves in the relegation zone. Despite all these difficulties, over 20,000 fans made the journey from Wrexham. They were rewarded with a 2–0 victory over Southend United. Along with the fans, I thoroughly enjoyed that day, and it reminded me what it is that I like about my broadcasting work for BBC Radio Wales. My summarising means that I can still keep in touch with the fans, players and management of the club I really love. It also gives me the opportunity to bump into big names from the world of football and entertainment. That day I talked to the Welsh broadcaster and entertainer Owen Money. He was his usual vibrant self, full of humour and fun. I also talked to the larger-than-life Peterborough United manager, Barry Fry, and wondered why he was at the match. The next season he signed Darren Ferguson, who played and scored that day. Perhaps that's the answer to my question.

As well as the great days at Northampton, the victory over Arsenal and the Freight Rover Trophy triumph in Cardiff, there have been days in the commentary box which have not been so happy. During the 1996–7 season, again under the leadership of Brian Flynn, Wrexham enjoyed a great run in the FA Cup. After victories over Colwyn Bay, Scunthorpe, West Ham, Peterborough United and Birmingham City, they found themselves in the quarter-finals for the third time in their history. Remarkably, their only home win had been in the first round replay against Colwyn Bay. All the other victories had been on opponents' grounds. They now found themselves drawn away once again, this time against fellow League Two team, Chesterfield. Wrexham began the game, which was televised, as strong favourites and there was huge belief in the town that, for the first time in their history, the club could make it to the semi-finals. Unfortunately, it was not to be, and a mix-up between goalkeeper Andy Marriott and defender Deryn Brace led to Chris Beaumont scoring Chesterfield's only goal. At the end of the game, I had to hide my great disappointment from the listeners. I had really expected something wonderful from the team that day, but unlike their performances in previous rounds, they did not play well and deserved to lose a scrappy game.

My other great disappointment came at the end of the 2010–11 season. After three seasons out of the Football League playing in the Blue Square Premier, they reached the play-off finals. Before the first leg at the Racecourse, I had already suffered a minor disappointment. Originally I had thought that if Wrexham got to the final, then they would be playing at Wembley. I daydreamed about summarising from the new state-of-the-art stadium. Unfortunately, a few weeks before the end of the season, it was announced that it would be held at Manchester City's stadium. It didn't really have the same appeal, although as events turned out, I needn't have dreamed or worried. The first leg was played at the Racecourse in front of a good crowd of over 7,000. Sadly the tie was over after thirty minutes, by which time Luton Town were in a commanding 3–0 lead which they protected until the final whistle. The Hatters were brilliant on the night and deserved their victory. In the second leg, the possibility of reaching the Football League seemed totally impossible. Perhaps because of that, Wrexham played with a far greater freedom, as if they had nothing to lose. They took an early lead and were then awarded a penalty. Had Gareth Taylor converted the spot kick instead of missing, then the outcome may have been very different. In the end the Reds lost 1–2, an aggregate defeat of 1–5.

I really enjoy the camaraderie that I have built up with members of the radio team. In many ways it is like an extension of the friendship and team spirit I enjoyed as a footballer. I often share journeys with Dylan Griffiths, who commentates for the Welsh-language station, Radio Cymru. I enjoy working with the many different commentators, but particularly look forward to sharing the airwaves with Rob Phillips. He is a wonderful character, famous for wearing his peak cap whether the sun is shining, it's raining or snowing. I consider him a good friend and colleague, but then everyone I work with at Radio Wales is fantastic.

I have a fairly fixed routine when I am summarising. I try to arrive at the ground for 1.30 p.m. (for a 3 p.m. kick-off) and would normally be away by about 6 p.m. I have to prepare a brief analysis before kick-off, which can last from thirty seconds to three minutes. In addition, I'm expected to give an assessment of the game at half-time and at full-time and then, after that final whistle, I record a match report which will be broadcast the next day on sports bulletins.

If Wrexham are playing away, I try to leave home by 9 a.m. Having been a professional footballer who has spent many hours of my life on coaches, long journeys don't bother me. Although, I have to admit that the journey to Boston, Lincolnshire is something else. That has to be the longest and furthest journey I've made there and back in a day.

Once I'm at the ground, whether it's the Racecourse

or away, I am excited, not just because I am looking forward to the match. There is always an uncertainty about who I am going to meet that day. When I was with the commentary team at Upton Park for Wrexham's Cup match against West Ham United, the first person I bumped into was Jimmy Armfield. A great player in his day, with Blackpool and England, he is now a summariser with Radio Five Live and still the perfect gentleman. And then there is always the chance that I will end up chatting with players and mangers from my own playing past, another reason why I love my work for Radio Wales so much.

10

Taking stock of it all

THERE IS LITTE doubt that since I was playing in the 1960s, '70s and '80s, football has changed a great deal. One of the major differences is the attitude of players and managers to injuries. My experiences of being told to head the ball on the good side of my head, or just kick, don't head it, would never happen today. Nor would a player with a serious neck injury be hoisted up onto the bar and then lifted back up if he fell off. Looking back I realise that I could easily have been paralysed. It's all personal fitness regimes these days, and very little sign of the old bucket of water and the magic sponge.

When I was playing there was a lot more bravado amongst players. It was a harsher, tougher game. Tackles were not outlawed as they are in today's game. At the beginning of a match I knew that the first time I received the ball, I would end up on the deck – the player marking me was letting me know that he was there. The player who kicked me the most was the great Paddy Crerand, the Manchester United right half. When I played against him for Northampton Town in the FA Cup, I admired his silky skills but I wasn't so keen on his clattering tackles.

My other fierce tackling foe was John McGrath, who played for Southampton. John used to roll up his shorts and, as a striker, when you saw him do that, you just knew you were in for a rough old afternoon. It was not nasty and you never felt that the defender was trying to break your leg. If you got scythed down from the back, you just picked yourself up and got on with the game.

Nowadays, when players go down after a tackle they beat the ground with their fists or else they writhe in agony. Then, they leap up and wave an imaginary card at the referee and try to get their opponent sent off. Very often the entire team will crowd around the official to influence his decision. There are too many cheats in the game and it makes the referee's job very difficult.

It's not just the players who try to influence the way a game develops. The crowd can also play a huge part and there are times when the atmosphere inside a stadium is almost gladiatorial. When they see one of their players on the ground, they often rise as a man to chant, "Cheat, cheat, cheat", or "Off, off, off". All of this must influence the referee.

Despite modern officials clamping down on the tackle, when the action is in the penalty area, they seem to take a much more relaxed attitude. When the ball is sent into the box from a corner kick, you can almost hug and kiss your opposite number. Players can be all over each other, yet nothing is ever given. I suppose it makes the game flow more but I find it strange how that physical contact, which was frowned upon in my playing days, is allowed, yet tackles are not.

I think outlawing the tackle has affected derby matches. They were once full-blooded affairs with tackles flying in right, left and centre. Personally, I think fans enjoy strong tackling. Today's derby matches so often turn out to be insipid affairs and a big yawn.

When I was playing, diving in the opponent's box to try and get a penalty and put the defender in the referee's book, or get him sent off, was becoming more commonplace in the game. Frannie Lee of Manchester City was one of the worst culprits. But, compared to all the gamesmanship of many of today's footballers, what Frannie got up to was fairly mild.

It was not just bravado which made the players of my era take the rough stuff without complaint. There were also financial considerations. Very often, on top of your basic wage, you would get a £20 bonus every time you played, so-called appearance money. At that time, £20 was a good sum of money, which meant that if you were carrying an injury you would try to hide it from the manager. You would hope that you could shake off whatever injury you had before the next game, so that you would get your bonus.

Just as many of the tackles were all about mind games, I think a lot of football was as much about psychology and physicality rather than skill. When I was a striker, I always wanted to take the penalties. A lot of players shrink away from the responsibility of taking the spot kick, but I always had the confidence to have a go. Besides, as a striker, I always aimed to score at least twenty goals a season for my team. If I could bag five from the spot, then that meant I would only need to score another fifteen from open play to reach the target. Taking penalties is a real battle of the mind and the ex-Liverpool goalkeeper, Bruce Grobbelaar, was a master at unsettling the penalty taker with his exploits on the goal line. For me, it was always a case of knowing in my mind where I was going to send the ball as a I ran up to the spot. I would constantly be thinking about planting the ball and would never allow thoughts about the goalie to enter my mind. I would always side-foot the penalty to the keeper's right which is where most left-footers send them. On one occasion John Sillett told me to change my style. He felt that my penalties were too predictable and encouraged me to hit it hard and place it to the goalkeeper's left. I tried that a few times, but I would say that 90 per cent of my penalties were side-footed to the goalkeeper's right.

In all my league appearances I never missed a penalty. In fact, I only missed two in my entire career and they were both in Cup ties, one against Norwich City in the League Cup and the other against Newport County when I was playing for Corby Town. In that game against the south Walians, which ended in a 3–3 draw, I scored a hat-trick but couldn't make it four from the penalty spot. The only time I felt pressure as I took a penalty was when I was playing for Wrexham in the Second Division. It was near the end of the season and we had been dragged into the relegation fight. We needed to beat a team who were also in the relegation zone. A victory would mean that we were safe. As I stepped up to do my famous side-footer to the goalie's right, I felt pressure for the first time – real pressure. I shot, scored and we were safe.

As I compare football today to the time when I was playing, I realise that the game is now played in a totally different way. At almost every level, the play now goes through the middle and wingers have very nearly disappeared. It is all a case of pass and move.

There are one or two wingers in the Premier League, but they don't play every week. They are now a luxury. If a team is facing a hard game against tough opposition, then the manager would not think of fielding an out-and-out winger. He would select an extra midfielder and play five across the middle.

One of the major changes in football is the team formation. The only position which seems to be a constant is the goalkeeper. When I was playing you would have a right back and left back in front of the keeper and a centre half lining up ahead of the two defenders. The right half and left half would be the two midfielders and then you would have an attacking force of five players. Outside right and outside left would be the wingers with a centre forward and an inside right and inside left either side of him. If you had to put that formation in numbers it would probably be the Two-One-Two-Five formation. Nowadays most teams favour a Four-Five-One structure, with just one striker up front on his own. I think for that line-up to work you have to have talented players, and it certainly makes for an exciting game in the Premiership, where most teams are full of great players from other countries. Many of the teams in the lower divisions can struggle to make their football exciting and eye-catching. But teams like Manchester United, under the brilliant Alex Ferguson, still play a very beautiful game.

As I have been writing this story of my footballing life, two very different Wrexham worlds have been existing next to each other and, at times, fighting each other. In the one world there is the Wrexham team, which again and again defied the odds by beating the might of top flight opposition such as Arsenal, Newcastle United,

Nottingham Forest, Southampton and nine other top teams. A club that could defeat Porto, the European Champions and, under my management, push Real Zaragoza all the way in a two-leg tie. A town that, although one of the smallest to have a professional football club, could produce a team that rose to the second tier of the Football League and *stayed* there for four seasons. A world in which Wrexham were watched by crowds of over 20,000 at the Racecourse and by over 40,000 at St James' Park Newcastle for an FA Cup tie against Blyth Spartans. This Wrexham had great players such as Mickey Thomas, Joey Jones, Bobby Shinton, Dai Davies, John Roberts, Les Cartwright, Arfon Griffiths, Alan Dwyer, Micky Evans, Mel Sutton and Graham Whittle. They were hailed by Bill Shankly as the best team he had ever seen outside the First Division. I was fantastically privileged to be part of that Wrexham world, helping the club into the Second Division for the first and only time in its history. It was a world full of excited and raucous fans, thrilled to be part of the dream rise of a small club from nowhere to the big time.

It has been wonderful to write about that world and it has given me joy to relive many unforgettable moments. But all the time I have been writing, there has been another world clamouring for my attention. In that other world Wrexham Football Club no longer frighten teams like Fulham or West Ham, or embarrasses Arsenal and Porto. Sadly, that other world is the real world, the world of 2011 when each day news on the radio, television and in newspapers tells me of the latest disaster to strike the club. I have been writing this book against the backcloth of one potential buyer for the club after another, pulling out. It has been strange to write a book, a large part of which is about my time at and my love for Wrexham Football Club, and to be wondering at the same time whether or not there will still be a club there by the time the book is published.

Since about 2004 the club has lurched from one crisis to the next. Whilst would-be asset strippers, such as Hamilton and Gutterman have not helped, I am convinced that the lack of contracts for players has caused many of Wrexham's problems. In seasons of financial difficulties, the club has always been able to make money by selling its best players. When I was the manager, I was able to bring the debt down from £350,000 to £115,000 through the sale of players such as Barry Horne, Mike Hooper, Jim Steel, Shaun Cunnington and Kevin Russell. With footballers now free to go where they like, it is no longer an option to make money through the sale of players. In the lower leagues you just have to carry the debts and hope for the best. For years, directors have dipped into their own pockets to bail Wrexham out of trouble. The events of 2010–11 have taught us that that can no longer continue.

As the new season dawned in August 2011, it struck me that there was turmoil off the field, but not on it. Dean Saunders seemed to have assembled a group of players ready to fight for the cause. Optimism was high that the club could once again reach the play-offs and might even win the Championship and therefore a direct route back into the Football League. Throughout the summer months it had seemed that the owners, Geoff Moss and Ian Roberts, would sell the club to the Supporters' Trust. Unfortunately, disputes emerged between the old and potential owners. This resulted in the owners refusing to pay the wages of the players.

The players responded by saying that if they were not being paid they would not play.

After a promising performance in a pre-season game at the Racecourse against Premiership outfit Wolverhampton Wanderers, manager Dean Saunders suddenly found himself with no team to field for a friendly match away to Colwyn Bay. Whilst I find it difficult to defend such action, I do have sympathy for the players. Many of them have young families to support and mortgages to pay. At that time they were unclear about their individual futures and were afraid of playing for nothing in case they sustained injuries which could jeopardise their future careers.

With all the financial upheaval, a new consortium appeared on the horizon. Headed by Alan Bermingham, who had played for Wrexham in the late 1960s and early 1970s and containing several businessmen, they were keen to take over if the Supporters' Trust failed. Some of the uncertainty disappeared when Glyndŵr University bought the ground and the players were eventually paid.

Just eight days before the start of the new season, I heard on the BBC Wales news that the League had said that Wrexham would have to pay a bond of £250,000 by 5 p.m. the following Monday or else they would not be allowed to compete in the Blue Square Bet Premier League. This basically suggested that the club which had meant so much to me could fold within days.

Throughout that day hundreds of fans called at the Racecourse to give cash donations or to pay money into the club's bank account. One of the first through the gate was a ten-year-old boy who donated his savings of

£35. I also heard of a gentleman who offered the deeds of his house. Throughout all the time that I have been associated with Wrexham Football Club, the fans have been terrific. Their response on that day and the weeks surrounding the new season, went far beyond the call of duty. Before the D-Day of that Monday in August, fans had collected money on the streets for the Supporters' Trust and some fans organised a sponsored walk. They left the Turf Hotel car park, just outside the football ground, at 4 a.m. on a Saturday and then walked to Northwich for the friendly match against Northwich Victoria, many of them arriving just thirty minutes before kick-off.

I think the tremendous support of the fans has galvanised the players on the field. Not only have they pulled through the period of no wages, but they have also survived the shock departure of Dean Saunders, ten games into the season. Having watched most of the games last season and several this, for BBC Radio Wales, I believe they are playing a far better style of football and they are more attacking. In the past, if they were leading by one goal they would try and sit on their lead and protect the score. That would often result in the match ending in a draw or Wrexham losing the game. This season, the players are playing with a freedom and confidence which makes them hungry to go on and score more goals and win by a greater margin.

As I write we are fourteen games into the 2010–11 season and the results have been terrific. Wrexham sit on top of the table, two points clear of the chasing teams after becoming the first team to defeat leaders Gateshead on their own turf. It was not just a victory, far more a demolition, as Wrexham won 4–1 and could easily have scored ten. They have also beaten two of the teams pundits tipped for honours before the season started: Fleetwood Town and Kidderminster Harriers were both beaten at the Racecourse by the same scoreline of 2–0.

While they have excelled against some of the stronger sides, they sometimes struggle against those near the foot of the table. In the game before their swaggering performance at Gateshead, they had to battle hard to beat lowly Ebbsfleet 1–0 at the Racecourse. They often play better away from home. It is sometimes easier when you haven't got the pressure of a large home crowd expecting you to win. It is also the case that in this league, many of the visiting teams see the Racecourse as their Cup final. They sit with ten men behind the ball and it is hard to break them down. As the home team, you have to move them around to find the gaps and you also need to control the tempo.

After ten games of the 2011–12 season and just a few days before the away game at Grimsby, Dean Saunders was unveiled as the new manager of Championship team Doncaster Rovers. It was inevitable that Dean would accept the offer to manage a team three divisions above Wrexham. As a manger you only get one such chance, and despite the fact that Wrexham were so well placed in their league, it was no surprise when he accepted the job. The only astonishing element in the move was that no one knew it was happening until it was all done and dusted.

Andy Morrell was entrusted with the role of caretaker manager for four games. His tenure finished with the victory at Gateshead and I would be very surprised if he is not installed as the permanent manager. He is the fans' favourite for all his goal-scoring exploits for the club, before he joined Championship team, Coventry City. Normally when a new manager takes over, he joins a club that is enduring poor results and struggling. Andy has been fortunate to take over at a time when the club is flying high.

In the brief time Andy has been in charge he has made one tactical change which has already succeeded. He has taken Lee Fowler from the midfield position in front of the back four and has put Dean Keates there. Lee has joined Jay Harris further up the field and this has given the team much more scope going forward.

To make Morrell the permanent manager seems the right move. He has the support of the players and supporters. It will also help the Supporters' Trust, as they run the finances of a club which possesses few resources. If they do appoint internally then they will not have to find a huge salary to replace Dean Saunders with a manager from outside the club.

The Supporters' Trust were given 26 September as a deadline by which they had to complete buying the club. The owners said that if the forms were not signed by the end of trading on that day, then they would look for alternative buyers. Mercifully, the Trust completed, and as a former player and an ardent fan I wish them well. They now await ratification from the League that everything is in order, and I hope that they will receive this quickly.

Once again there is hope. The Supporters' Trust are determined to cut the budget and I believe they are right. There is a need for the club to work with what they have, and not overstretch themselves financially. Other clubs have been in a similar plight and survived. In 2003,

Swansea City had to win their last game of the season to remain in the Football League. They beat Hull City and under Kenny Jackett and Roberto Martinez, steadily climbed up the divisions into the Championship. Then, in the play-off final in 2011, they defeated Reading to go into the Premiership for the first time in their history. AFC Wimbledon have also resurrected themselves from the grave and in 2011 they began life as a League Two side.

It took a long time for both Swansea City and AFC Wimbledon to turn things around. And as fans, players and management enter a new period of hope at Wrexham Football Club, it is vital that everyone is patient. While we are desperate for them to get back into the Football League, we have to realise that if in 2014 we are still in the Blue Square Premier League but are solvent, then that will be a positive outcome, as we shall still have a football club.

I, for one, am optimistic. Four thousand people often watch the club at non-league level. The fans proved in 2010–11 how brilliantly dedicated they were by raising money to keep the club alive. In the next three years I hope that, as well as moving up through the leagues, the club will have a great Cup run. Manchester United away in the Cup would solve a lot of financial problems. I live in hope that this club, which has given me so much and which I love so dearly, will rise again.

When I think about the Wrexham fans I always feel humbled. They are so loyal and committed – not just when facing the kind of problems the club endured at the beginning of the 2010–11 season, but in their reaction to players such as me. When I finished my playing career and talked to the chairman about the possibility of a testimonial match, he told me that there would be no problem. It is always a great privilege for a player to be given a testimonial game.

I was thrilled by the club's response, but there was now the slight problem of which team to approach. I suppose like almost every football fan in the Wrexham area, I immediately thought of Manchester United. I didn't know Sir Alex, but I thought nothing ventured, nothing gained. I rang Old Trafford. He was not available but I was told that the great man would ring me back. I enjoyed telling my two sons, Richard and Jamie, "If anyone rings for me, it'll be Sir Alex Ferguson, just tell him I'll call back later." They couldn't believe it and neither could I when, a couple of hours later, I picked up the phone to hear Sir Alex returning my call. He was extremely friendly and chatty, but apologetic that the club had three friendly matches lined up for that season, so they were unable to help.

I had a similar response from David Moyes at Everton, and Liverpool were already committed to coming to the Racecourse in the following pre-season. At that time, one of the most exciting teams to watch in the top division was Newcastle United. Again, I didn't know their manager, but I left a message for Kevin Keegan and forty-eight hours later he replied.

So it was that 6,000 fans turned out to see a star-studded side play Wrexham in my testimonial match. Given that our attendances rarely exceeded 2,000 it was a fantastic response. I am so grateful to them for their support of me and perhaps this book is my way of saying "Thankyou" to all those who have made me feel part and parcel of the town of Wrexham. I have been here for thirty-five years, and the way I feel about the place and its people, I might as well have been born here.

APPENDIX

My footballing life in a nutshell

Born 6 January 1947 in Melton Mowbray, Leicestershire.

1964–6: I sign for First Division club Leicester City and go from earning £2.7s.6d. a week to £25 a week. At the end of my second year I am devastated to be told that I am no longer required. (see chapter 1)

1966–7: Jock Basford signs me for Fourth Division Exeter City. I make my debut in a 0–0 draw at the Racecourse against Wrexham. But despite 11 goals in 31 appearances, manager Frank Broome releases me.

I marry Dana 2 January 1967.

1967–9: I play part-time football for Corby Town and combine football and work. The next season, Fourth Division Northampton Town sign me for £5,000. (see chapter 2)

1969–70: Northampton Town have a good Cup run and reach the fifth round of the FA Cup and lose 2–8 to Manchester United. George Best scores six and I get one.

1971–2: In a pre-season friendly I fracture my skull. The manager, Dave Bowen, tells me to head the ball on the side of the head that doesn't hurt. In January 1972 I sign for Lincoln City and end the season with 27 goals.

1972–3: I finish as top scorer at Lincoln City with 21 goals.

1973–4: Top scorer again for Lincoln City with 19 goals. I ask manager Graham Taylor for a pay rise but end up on the transfer list. Hereford United sign me for £15,000 with a promise of another £5,000 if I score 20 goals. (see chapter 3)

Our first son Richard is born.

1974–5: I score 32 goals for Hereford and am voted Player of the Season by the fans and win the Rothman's Golden Boot award for finishing as the highest scorer in all four divisions of the Football League.

1975–6: Hereford United are promoted to the Second Division for the first time in their history. I score 37 goals and win the Golden Boot award and am top scorer in all four divisions again.

1976–7: Hereford United are relegated and I sign for Wrexham for £60,000. (see chapter 4)

1977–8: Wrexham are champions of the Third Division and are promoted to the Second Division for the first time in their history. I score 24 goals in 23 appearances. (see chapter 5)

1978–9: Arctic weather conditions disrupt our season and we are unable to play a league game for two months. Our FA Cup match with Stockport County is cancelled nine times.

In November our second son Jamie is born.

1979–80: Wrexham fans vote me Player of the Year and I score 20 goals. My record of scoring in ten consecutive FA Cup ties (which still stands) comes to an end in our 2–5 defeat to Everton in the fifth round.

I also set a club record of scoring in eleven consecutive home games. My goal against Chelsea is selected for December's Goal of the Month on *Match of the Day*. (see chapter 6)

1980–1: Wrexham beat FA Cup holders West Ham United in the third round of the FA Cup after three attempts. We secure our Second Division status, but only 3,220 come to watch us. Arfon Griffiths resigns as manager and Mel Sutton replaces him.

1981–2: I make my 500th league appearance against Leicester City. Reigning European Champions Nottingham Forest are beaten 3–1 away in the third round of the FA Cup. I fracture my cheek bone and miss thirteen league games. Wrexham are relegated to the Third Division. (see chapter 7)

1982–3: The Wrexham chairman tells me the club can no longer afford me and I play my last game for Wrexham at home to Exeter City on 9 October 1982. I sign for Fourth Division Hereford United but decide to retire soon afterwards. I play my last ever Football League game on 3 January 1983 in a 2–1 victory over Aldershot at Edgar Street.

1983–4: I concentrate on my business which makes fireplaces from natural stone at Minera, near Wrexham.

I play amateur football for Chirk AAA in the Welsh National League and for the Fairfield Tavern in the Sunday League. I start summarising Wrexham's matches for Radio Wales' sports programmes.

1984–5: I am appointed as Wrexham manager with three games of the season remaining.

1985–6: Wrexham win the Welsh Cup. I end up using six different goalkeepers in the season. And, at 37 years of age I play the last twenty minutes of an FA Cup replay at home to Notts County, because I have no other players to use.

1986–7: We reach the second round of the European Cup Winners' Cup and draw 2–2 at home against Real Zaragoza in front of 14,000 fans. However, a home match against Southend United is watched by only 900 people, a club record.

1987–8: To balance the books I have to sell top players. Despite a good finish (eleventh) our crowds for the season are the fourth worst in the entire Football League.

1988–9: Wrexham reach the play-offs. We beat Scunthorpe United 5–1 in the semi-final. In the final we draw 0–0 at home. In the second leg, with nine minutes to go, we are drawing 1–1 and on our way to the Third Division, but Leyton Orient score, and break our hearts. (see chapter 8)

1989–90: I resign as manger of Wrexham. John Sillett, now manager of Coventry City, asks me to join him as First Team Coach.

1990–1: John Sillett is sacked. I resign from Coventry City.

1994–5: Manager of Flint Town United in the Welsh League.

1999–2000: Manager of Caernarfon Town in the Welsh League. In a televised game we beat Swansea City in the quarter-final of the Welsh Premier Cup.

2004–7: I help my friends Ossie Jones and Graham Jones at Cefn Newi Druids in the Welsh League. (see chapter 9)

2010–11: I report on the dramatic events at Wrexham Football Club for BBC Radio Wales. (see chapter 10)

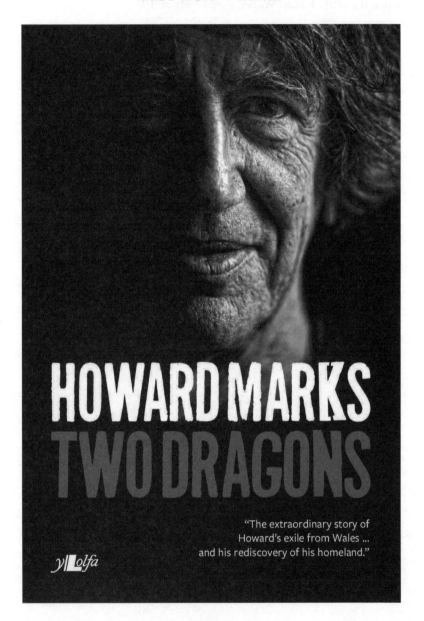

"A fierce Welsh nationalist, a friend of poets, midgets, gangsters and psychopathic wrestlers – Orig Williams had a remarkable journey."

EL BANDITO
ORIG WILLIAMS
THE AUTOBIOGRAPHY

y Lolfa

£9.95

Dixie is just one of a whole range of
publications from Y Lolfa. For a full list of
books currently in print, send now for your
free copy of our new full-colour catalogue.
Or simply surf into our website

www.ylolfa.com

for secure on-line ordering.

TALYBONT CEREDIGION CYMRU SY24 5HE
e-mail ylolfa@ylolfa.com
website www.ylolfa.com
phone (01970) 832 304
fax 832 782